ⓧ TIME FOR DIREC

WHY
WON'T YOU LET

ME
SPEAK?

Learn the vital communication skills for women
in the workplace. The dos and don'ts when
communicating with men and with each other!

By Sara G Harling

WHY

WON'T YOU LET

ME

SPEAK?

Learn vital communication skills for women in the work place. The do's and don'ts when communicating with men and each other!

By Sara G Harling

Dedication

This book is dedicated to every woman who wants to be listened to and feel she can speak up and be heard, and to all the women who wish to have fabulous lives feeling confident and proud of who they are, all that they are achieving and who they are becoming.

It doesn't matter what position you are in at work or what age you are. If you're finding communication hard with your colleagues, family or friends, whether they are male or female, then this book is for you.

These books are dedicated to all those who want to learn and grow in the quickest way possible.

Finally, I dedicate this book to my dad, who taught me that "There's always a way." No matter what we face in life, no matter the circumstances or problem, there is always a way to solve it and work everything out. I also dedicate this book to Rob, my partner, who challenges me, holds me accountable and has helped to influence me to write this book inspired by all that we have learned together at work, with colleagues and with each other.

Time for Direct Talk

Time for Direct Talk is a series of books that help empower you to learn new skills quickly. The books are written in a style that gets straight to the point—no fluff, just direct talk. We all have so many other responsibilities in our lives as well as our careers, and we don't have time to sit down to read 60,000 words when there is so much going on. We don't need to read 100 words when the same thing can be said in ten, so my mission with this range of books is to quickly, easily and effectively give you the tools you need without taking hours of your time. The Time for Direct Talk books will focus on key points that give you the tools to quickly learn how to adapt, implement and challenge your ways of working for rapid results.

Welcome to the first book from Direct Talk.

Book Review

Sara really understands the different aspects when communicating with men and women at work; this new book is a great self help guide and makes you reflect on how you can improve the way you communicate. There are helpful hints, practical exercises and working through the book I realised just how helpful and insightful it will be in giving me the tools to be a much better communicator.

—Amanda Batham
AJB Consultancy Services.

I read and reread this book, and read it to my sisters and daughter and mother! All ages agreed it was thought provoking, insightful and honest. I really wish you all the success with this and we certainly need to learn these tools to deal with the challenges we face everyday as women in the workplace and indeed in our personal lives too.

—Joe Bailey
Head of Farming, RSPCA Assured.

This is an informative, straight-talking and easy-to-read guide on the huge topic of communication. Not only has it enabled me to reflect on my past behaviours in the workplace (and in my personal life!), it's given me an insight into how others feel and act, as well as a suite of useful tools to employ going forward. I'm looking forward to putting what I've learned into practice!

—Kath Swinglehurst
Apple Tree Communications

This book is a great idea to condense so much information with so many tools that will now help me in so many areas of my work but in all areas of my personal life too; it's a must read!

—Sharan Madeley
Company Secretary, NHS

It's a game changer!

—Fiona Chamberlain
International Trade Advisor

This book has some really good debates in it and really makes you think about your own behaviour, the behaviour of others and challenges your own values and beliefs; keep reading to the end and it will change your life!

—Anonymous.

Contents

INTRODUCTION

Why Won't They Let Me Speak?

"I feel overlooked, unheard and uninvolved!"

Have you ever felt that way? Sat in a room with people and wanted to talk, but for some reason, you couldn't get a word in edgeways? You open your mouth to speak, but, as you do, someone starts speaking before you. Or you're in a meeting, and, as you're talking, someone else starts to talk over you, interrupts you and takes over the conversation. Ouch! Do you spend time overthinking and wondering why this keeps happening again and again and how it affects your confidence? Do you feel like no one is listening and like you can't be heard?

Then *stop!*

This book will give you tools and tips to help improve your communication skills quickly and effectively and boost your confidence in any situation.

> *There's always a way, and you always have a choice*

"Why won't they let me speak?" I have asked this question many times throughout my career—in fact, sometimes I've asked it in other situations too, with family, friends and loved ones. Ever been in a situation at home

1

where you're trying to engage with a loved one but you can't get a word in edgeways? The tension builds up, and, before you know it, you're having an argument. It's probably due to the same cause: lack of communication.

I love to learn, so throughout my career, I've been on many courses all over the world to learn about psychology and behaviour, and the results I have seen have been incredible. I want to share them with you in this book. Most importantly, as you will find out, what I have learned is simple to understand and easy to implement.

It isn't just about asking the person you are speaking to why *they* won't let you speak; it's also about asking yourself why *you* won't let yourself speak. Because most of the time, that is really the number one cause: *you!* That, for me, was quite a profound realisation when I was writing this book. I suddenly realised that this book isn't just about the problems in communication we are having with others; 80% of the time, the real issue is the communication we are having with ourselves, our conversations and the thoughts in our own minds along with our own behaviour.

The most important part of communication is constantly learning about and reflecting on how you communicate. It's understanding how you communicate to yourself and how you communicate to others. As we go through this book, we will cover both areas: 1) Why won't *you* let me speak? and 2) Why won't I let *myself* speak?

When talking with clients, interviewing many other women and men and reflecting on my own life experiences, I concluded that communication is also our own responsibility. If we face obstacles, rude people, discrimination and other challenges, we should reflect inwards as to how we can connect with them better, handle situations differently and communicate what we want in order to get the result we're looking for in any situation.

Communication is one of the most important aspects of our lives. It affects everything we do and everything we try to achieve, and it impacts the quality of our lives. It affects how we feel, how we make others feel and how we direct all areas in our lives, including work, family, friends and ourselves.

I'm by no means an expert, but I have spent the last thirty years dealing with communication at work, presenting on stage and communicating in teams and relationships. I've been nervous, said the wrong thing, reacted too soon and not reacted quickly enough. I've been frustrated, upset and emotional. I've been angry when certain situations have happened, and sometimes, I have even wondered why I bother to try. I've spent my career in sales, customer service, operations and high-level management. I've worked with different cultures, in large private businesses and small family companies. I have dealt with gender inequality, sexism, discrimination and many other issues at work and at home. I've been married, divorced, a mum, a step-mum, a manager, a director and a shop assistant, so I've covered nearly every situation in my career, and now I'm a coach and consultant. It doesn't matter what role you have; communication is the most important skill you can learn.

Can you imagine how creative and empowered children would be if they knew the power of their own minds? Communication, whether good or bad, affects every single aspect of life, love, work, health and relationships. It is a life skill that everyone should have.

There's no wonder there are problems in the world and in our lives— with health, crime, mental health, anxiety and depression, and relationships—when we don't know how to communicate! I hope to be able to give people the information and tools to understand and take back control of their lives for more empowering, happy and exciting lives ahead.

Learning how to communicate with yourself and others—whether that be with your partner, your children, your colleagues or your family and friends—is the first step to changing your life. I certainly would have made some different decisions if I had known some of the things that I'm about to teach you.

So why does it feel so hard for a woman to communicate at work, to feel fulfilled in her job? How does she create and maintain the desire to grow her career when there can be so many obstacles in the way? Why are so many women unhappy? One in three women says that they feel they are under a huge amount of stress with never-ending to-do lists. Some women don't particularly want a career per se; they just want to enjoy being at work. And why is that such a difficult thing to ask for? Is being a woman the main obstacle? Absolutely not.

Nearly all problems in work and in life begin and end around communication. Communication brings connection or disconnection. It changes how we feel, how we react and how we challenge each other; it affects the way that we respond, and it can be very different between men and women.

I learnt how to communicate effectively so that I could live my life, support others in theirs and eventually have the courage to write this book. I feel passionate about helping people understand that you do have a choice, a choice to learn to do things differently, to live a life without that stress and frustration when you feel like you are not heard or understood. I wanted to write this book to help others deal with communication, especially in the workplace and at home, and also to help others learn how to communicate with themselves so they can live the best version of their lives, to unleash their own full potential. In this book, we will also explore areas of communication that can make us feel frustrated, overwhelmed, disappointed and, at times, angry. We will discuss how to challenge situations such as sexism and discrimination that still exist in the workplace and society today. Let's face it: sexist comments, jokes and some behaviours will never go away completely— we are indeed two different sexes, after all—but how should we deal with these things? How do we speak up? This book will tell you.

There have been so many reports all over the world about the problems women face in the workplace, at home and in society. Progress is being made from where we were even ten years ago, but it feels slow, and now, with the effects of COVID-19, all the progress made could indeed be set back by years, according to the Women in Work Index 2021 report by PwC of London.

This is because those industries affected by COVID-19 were predominantly female-dominated industries, such as the accommodation and food services, and the art, entertainment, and recreation industries. In the UK, the Coronavirus Job Retention Scheme (CJRS) has meant that the pandemic's full impact on the labour market is yet to be seen, but if current furlough data is indicative of future unemployment trends, a larger number of women will face the risk of job loss than men once the scheme ends. It has never been more important to support women in work, help re-skill women, and challenge these behaviours and differences in all our lives.

Findings from The Global Gender Gap Index by the World Economic Forum are similar. The Index benchmarks the evolution of gender-based gaps among four key dimensions (Economic Participation and Opportunity, Educational Attainment, Health and Survival, and Political Empowerment) and tracks progress towards closing these gaps over time. This report came out just over a year after COVID-19 was officially declared a pandemic. Preliminary evidence suggests that the health emergency and the related economic downturn have impacted women more severely than men, partially reopening gaps that had already been closed.

Women need the support, the skills and the confidence in the workplace to return to work, enjoy their careers, and, if they want to, climb up that ladder. This is exactly what this book intends to do: give women the skills to succeed, not just in the workplace, but at home and in society as a whole. It all starts with communication.

In the next chapters, we will talk about the main factors that stop us from speaking up. It's time to learn how to deal with them and overcome any objections you may face.

Maybe you feel you can't speak up because you don't feel confident enough, or that someone else always controls the conversation so you don't get a word in edgeways. It might be that you are always interrupted every time you try and speak or get challenged and feel shot down in the process. There may be situations when you feel as though your emotions take over and you become embarrassed and red or even get a quiver in your voice, stutter or say the wrong thing. In each chapter, we will talk about why we feel we can't speak up, what the causes are and how to make the changes to stop that from happening. We will cover what's important, how to let go of what's not important and how to understand the difference.

Each chapter will give you the tools to feel confident and empowered so you can feel heard, understood and appreciated. We cover the "what ifs" in each section so you can understand how to overcome any situation you are faced with.

By the end of each chapter, you will be able to take the tools and implement them immediately in your life, making you feel more confident, happy and in control of what you want.

CHAPTER 1

What Is Communication?

Communicate means "to share," from the Latin word *communicare*. Communication is the process of giving information by verbal and non-verbal means.

Communication is the most fundamental critical skill we can learn in life. When you really think about it, you can see why I say this. You communicate with your family, your children, your friends, your colleagues, people you meet, your doctor, your dentist, your neighbours and, most importantly, yourself.

There are so many different aspects to communication skills that this book should be much longer, but I wanted this book to be short, sweet and to the point and to give you quick, easy-to-understand information with clear and concise steps to implement change. My goal was to help you understand what you can do to speak up and for your voice to be heard.

In this book, though, we are purely concentrating on the issues we face when we feel we can't speak up about communication issues between men and women in the workplace and the simple ways to address those issues. Communication is not just about words; there are types of communication and behaviour styles that either help you to communicate better or make your communication worse.

The thoughts we think and the words we speak influence our actions and those of everyone around us. If we think about a sad memory, we become sad in the moment, even emotional, as though it's real, even though the memory is from the past. Even a storyline in a movie can make us cry; it's not even real, but our thoughts are so strong that they connect deeply to our emotions and, before we know it, we're crying at a cartoon character who has lost the love of his life! The opposite is also true. Think of a time you were happy. What was going on? How did you feel? Really get into the detail of the memory and now, all of a sudden, your feelings start to change. Your body feels different, and your emotions turn from being sad to happy, all from a memory, all from changing your thoughts and changing your focus. How powerful is that? If we can change how we feel from a memory, we can change how we feel in the moment. When faced with a situation where you may feel nervous and anxious, remember a time when you felt confident and strong and then note how you start to feel different in your body. When you focus on feeling strong and confident, it's amazing that you actually start to feel it, just by focusing your thoughts on what you want and not on what you *don't* want.

> *Communication is a process of sharing information*

How we think and what we think affects the way we feel, and this, in turn, can dictate how we react, our decisions and actions, and, of course, our responses and the way we communicate.

If your own thoughts can cause this chain reaction in a memory, imagine how powerful you will feel knowing you can control them in the here and now. How much better can you communicate with yourself and how can you communicate with others, whether that be with your colleagues, in meetings or with your family? Your thoughts can either empower you or disempower you, which can indeed change your life now and for the future.

Let me give you an example. Now, this might sound daft, but when I do this, it transforms my immediate thoughts for the day.

> *Your thoughts either empower you or disempower you—you choose which!*

You wake up one morning and it's dark and raining. You're tired, and you just want to stay in bed. It takes three alarm snoozes to get you out of bed, and you drag your sorry ass to the bathroom. Your energy is low and you say to yourself, *God, what a crap morning. Rubbish weather, and it's so dark. I have a long day ahead with some boring meetings.* You open your wardrobe and put on a dark dress or suit and head down for breakfast, already thinking of everything that might go wrong during the workday ahead. You pour the coffee but spill the milk. You've run out of bread for your toast, and your children just finished off the cereal. There's nothing left for breakfast, and you then tell yourself, "I knew this was going to be a bad day!" You got what you focused on.

But imagine instead that the alarm goes off and you get out of bed and immediately give thanks for the fact that you're alive and have two feet on the ground! You say, "Good morning world, good morning butterflies, good morning birds, what a fabulous day it's going to be." Immediately, you're smiling, even though it is still dark, raining and still miserable outside. You're brushing your teeth thinking about your productive day ahead, now with optimism and hope. You have sticky notes of positive thoughts around your mirror and you read them whilst brushing your teeth. You open the wardrobe and, because of how you're feeling slightly uplifted, happier and more positive now, you choose that red dress instead of the black one and your mood lifts even higher. All things can change by just thinking a different thought; that is it!

Now you still won't have any milk and no bread for your toast, and it may still be raining but you will have a totally different attitude towards your day. Maybe those meetings won't be so boring after all!

Try it for yourself. Just the slightest shift in your thoughts can completely change the way you feel!

I also do this when driving. I once read a story about how we never know what's going on in someone else's life and how we should never be quick to judge, and that story has stayed with me forever. A man once sat on a train and another, younger man got on the train at the next stop with his three sons. The younger man seemed like he was being a bit distant towards his sons, who were loud, climbing up and off the chairs, running around and screaming. This went on for five to ten minutes, disturbing all the rest of the passengers.

The older man turned to the younger man and said, "Don't you think you'd better stop your boys from shouting and running around?"

The younger man responded, "Yes, I should, really. The thing is, I don't know what to do and I guess they also don't know what to do. You see, we have just come from the hospital where their mother has just died!"

That story just stopped me dead in my tracks. How awful! And yes, you can see and understand why they were reacting in this way. What this story taught me was that whilst we can get upset and frustrated, even angry, at someone else's behaviour, that doesn't mean we have to react to it. I use this story every time someone has road rage or is driving on my bumper or cuts me off at traffic lights. I say to myself, *Sara, don't get mad. He could be rushing on his way to the hospital to visit someone in need.* This immediately changes my thoughts and in turn changes my feelings, and I no longer feel pressured, frustrated, mad or even angry. I certainly don't react. Before, I might have.

So, for sure, our thoughts control our feelings, our focus and our actions. Choose better thoughts that empower you and change situations or feelings to more positive ones.

I get to choose how to live my own life, on my terms. I get to choose my own thoughts, which means I choose my actions and my reactions and my feelings, and therefore I choose to be happier and healthier and live my best life. What a life lesson to know!

We can choose our own thoughts and beliefs, and this then dictates our feelings and our actions. Now, don't get me wrong, it takes practice and time to focus on this. Catch yourself in the moment as you have those negative thoughts and then change them to what you want them to be.

Communication is an expression of how we feel, our thoughts and our ideas, and we do this through spoken words, sounds, body language, written words and our behaviours. There are four types of communication: verbal, non-verbal, written and visual. Some people would say there is a fifth, which is listening.

In this book, we are only going to focus on communication that is done face-to-face. We will not be discussing written communication.

> *Your thoughts can either empower you or disempower you, which can change your life now and for the future.*

Verbal and Non-Verbal Communication

I want to introduce you to the 7% rule, if you don't already know it.

The theory was developed by psychology professor Albert Mehrabian at the University of California, Los Angeles, who did various studies that led him to conclude that when we communicate, only 7% is verbal (with words) and 93% is non-verbal. Of that non-verbal communication, 55% is body language and 38% is in our tone, pace and the volume of our voice. Non-verbal communication plays a very important part in how we communicate and how we come across to the receiver. We may use words to say something while our body language sends the opposite message to the receiver.

Verbal Communication

Words are powerful, and they influence our communication to either go in one direction or another. I saw a post one day on LinkedIn on why to stop saying sorry: "Sorry I'm late" or "Sorry I forgot." When you say "Sorry," it shows the other person that they were not important enough for you to do whatever you're apologising for, in this example, either a) being on time or b) remembering something you were supposed to do. Of course, saying "sorry" also makes you feel bad that you're late or that you forgot. However, if you switch "sorry" to "thank you," that completely changes the way it makes you and the other person feel. Change "Sorry I'm late" to "Thank you for waiting." Can you see the difference? You are being thankful to the other person for waiting for you and showing that you appreciate them for it. I think this is such a powerful way to change the emotion and feelings about how you being late can affect the other person. I mean, really always try to be on time in the first place. It's no excuse. But what a difference a few words can make! The same with "Sorry I forgot," which can make the person feel unimportant and insignificant, compared to "Thank you for reminding me," which now makes them feel appreciated rather than insignificant.

Always think about the words you choose to use. I use this as a constant reminder each day to reflect on my day and question if I could have chosen better words in the situations I've been in so that next time I can communicate better.

> *Stop saying "sorry" and start saying "thank you." Always remember that you don't know what someone else is going through.*

Non-Verbal Communication

Non-verbal communication is our tone, our pace, the volume at which we speak, our facial expression and posture, the way we hold our hands, the way we stand and sit, and even our image, such as the clothes we wear and our hair and makeup. It all communicates a message.

If we wear a suit as we leave the house, everyone receives the message that we are on our way to work, and, likewise, if we leave the house in our gym clothes and trainers, it can be assumed that we are going to do some exercise. It all sends out a message.

Have you ever tried to have a conversation with someone who stands with their hands on their hips, with raised eyebrows and a cold expression, compared to a person who stands in front of you with open arms and looks directly at you when you talk, with warm eyes that show that they are listening? There is a reason why Sheryl Sandberg calls her book *Lean In*! Leaning in shows that you are interested. Your body language tells people that you care, and it demonstrates that you want to listen and that you want to know or do more.

To ensure that the other person knows you are listening to them, check in with your own body language. Having your arms open in a relaxed manner suggests that you are open to listening to what they have to say. It makes the other person feel valued and important. Sit or stand in a comfortable way, but don't slouch. Put all your attention on the other person so that they can see in your face that you are interested in what they have to say. Be aware of your body language as you communicate various messages. You want to ensure you are giving the right message. In so many meetings, I look around the table and see people slouched in their seats, their heads resting in their hands as they gaze out of the window. Seriously, they couldn't make it any more obvious that they're not interested in the meetings! Body language is crucial because it gives out non-verbal messages that could be misunderstood by the other people involved, and this will set your conversations to go in the totally wrong direction. Even though you are using the correct words, the outcome due to your body language can be the total opposite of what you want to achieve.

Also, remember that you can learn a lot from the other person's body language. It can help you gauge what they are thinking and feeling, and then you can start to ask them questions around their non-verbal responses. For example, if they fold their arms as you are talking about a subject, that can be an indication that they are becoming closed in about the subject you are talking about. Maybe they are becoming defensive or feel vulnerable about the conversation, and at this point, you can ask questions to clarify how they are feeling and what they are thinking. Always bear in mind though that they may just feel more comfortable with their arms folded, and that's why you ask the questions—so you can clarify the non-verbal language they are communicating to you.

> *Be aware of your body language as you communicate various messages. You want to ensure you are giving the right message. Read your conversational partner's body language to gauge what they are communicating, too*

Your tone, pace and volume also show a communication style. A fast pace will of course convey a certain amount of energy and excitement, compared to a slow pace, which will come across with more compassion rather than excitement.

Since 38% of our communication comes through in our tone, be aware of just how you are talking. The volume and pace at which we speak both contribute to how our spoken word is communicated and received by the other person.

Communication Styles

Next, we need to understand that everyone is more dominant in how they communicate depending on whether they are visual, kinaesthetic, or auditory in their preferred approach to communication and connection. It's a learning style, and if someone learns in a certain way, they will also communicate in that style of learning. People will easily demonstrate this to you in the language they use.

For example, imagine you are talking to a team member at the office about the latest targets and she says, "I feel that the targets that Brian has given to us are way too high to achieve." You can connect to her by also using kinaesthetic language, such as, "He probably feels, after you did so well last month, that you can achieve more this month," or "I feel that way too, and if we work on our prospects a bit more, I bet we can do it."

Using the same sense to communicate back makes it feel as if you are both connected a little bit more than if you don't use the same sense, and that creates a stronger rapport.

Tony Robbins, in his course Mastering Influence, explains that we all have our communication styles, depending on our preferred way of learning.

If you want to learn more on this, there are many studies that go into more detail and break down the style of how we learn and communicate. The VARK model is a great start to help you begin to understand how people learn to then understand how they will communicate. It stands for visual, auditory, read/write and kinaesthetic. To learn more, go to www.vark-learn.com.

It's also important to say here that people communicate well with one another when they like the person with whom they are communicating.

We all have certain communication styles, either 1) visual, 2) auditory and 3) kinaesthetic. Your more dominant sense will dictate how you perceive, receive and communicate in a particular situation.

We all have five senses that we use to connect with the world around us: smell, taste, touch, sight and sound. In communication, we use sight, sound and touch—otherwise known as visual communication (learning best by seeing and reading), auditory communication (learning best by listening) and kinaesthetic communication (learning best through touch and doing).

> *We learn by being more visual, auditory or kinaesthetic; which one are you?*

We each have a more dominant sense that we use to interpret things around us. You can tell which sense you connect more to from the language you use. For example:

- "I *feel* the targets are too high this month."
- "It *sounds* like the targets are too high this month."
- "Can I *see* the target levels you want us to achieve compared to last month's?"

Once you realise which language a person uses, you can use the same type back to them. As examples:

- "I *feel* like the targets are too high this month."— "The targets may seem strong, and I *feel* you can easily achieve them."

- "It *sounds* like the targets are too high this month."— "I know it *sounds* like it, and your progression so far demonstrates your skills to reach them."
- "Can I *see* the target levels you wanted us to achieve compared to last month's?"— "Yes, here you go; you can *see* why we came up with these numbers based on last month's performance."

By communicating in the same style, you can connect far more easily, helping the other person to feel connected and showing that you understand them. They learn and understand better from you, enabling both of you to reach the desired outcome.

I once had to have a difficult conversation with a member of my team and couldn't seem to connect with him. He wanted to do things in a certain way for the team members he supervised, but it added time and restricted our ability to turn around projects quickly for our customers, and we were losing out to our competition.

I used examples to demonstrate this issue. I showed him different ways of doing things so that it was easy to understand, but no, "I'm not doing it," he said, and every time I brought the subject up, I could see he was ready for a fight about it. I was about to give up when I remembered this technique of connecting through learning styles.

I recognised that he had used the word "feel" throughout our conversations. "I *feel* that the process is open to mistakes, and I won't expose my team to *feeling* like they are responsible when anything goes wrong." That was a really fair and plausible reason for him to give me, but it still didn't help us get to market before our competitors..

So, I started to use the word "feel" as well. "Yes, I *feel* like you're right, and your team *feeling* concerned over changing things is understandable. What do you *feel* is the right thing to do so that we can get ahead of our competition?" And *boom*, off he went with some suggestions that indeed enabled us to change things and get ahead. We had been talking about this for months and months, and things had been starting to get difficult between us, but within minutes of my using this technique, we started to change things and brainstorm, and eventually, we got the right outcome.

This technique is also called mirror and matching. It's about copying the same body language and the same spoken language with your tone, your volume and your pace in order to establish a connection with the other person. If someone speaks at a slower pace than you, don't talk too quickly. Talk at their pace so that they connect with you. If the other person speaks quickly and loudly, do the same thing. It takes practice, but just start to be aware of these different things and then try them out, and you'll be amazed at how you can connect and communicate far better, more easily and more effectively when you do.

> *Mirror and matching is a powerful tool to connect with another person.*

Left Brain vs. Right Brain

Our brains come into play too, as we will all be more dominant on one side of our brains than the other. The left brain and right brain theory was created in the 1960s by a psychologist called Roger W. Sperry.

A person can either be right-brained or left-brained. That means that one side of the brain is dominant. Left-brain-dominant people are methodical and analytical in nature. Those who are right-brain dominant are creative and artistic. This information in itself helps us to connect with people, as, if you can tell someone is more logical than creative in the way they present themselves, you can then tailor your conversation to how they express themselves in order to create rapport.

This is very similar to what I mentioned earlier about choosing words that empower and connect to others during conversation. If you know someone is more logical than creative, show them the facts rather than how you are going to achieve something. If that person is more creative, then start by showing them how they will achieve it rather than showing them the facts behind it. The way in which we say things is so powerful; this even more so when you are stuck in the middle of an argument. This is why listening is far more powerful than talking!

Deductive and Inductive Thinkers

Another point to consider is the notion from authors Ethan Becker and Jon Wortmann's *Mastering Communication at Work* that listeners (whether male or female) are either deductive or inductive and that they respond to the kind of communication that matches their natural tendency.

Deductive thinkers want the point and the details that support it first, and inductive thinkers need to hear the details first before they can consider the point. Analysis needs to be done to establish whether this is a female or male trait, but in the research I have done so far, it certainly does seem that females are more likely to be inductive than males.

When presenting or talking to colleagues at work, it can be worth finding out which method they prefer before talking to them. You can either work this out by watching how they communicate or by simply asking them. "John, in the presentation tomorrow, do you prefer to understand the reasons behind the growth plan for the next quarter or just the bullet points?"

Do they like detail or just bullet points? Do you need to get to the point of giving a detailed explanation, or do you need to explain the full background to your conclusion? We all know that person who uses 200 words when most of us can say the same thing in just 20—which, by the way, is the very reason behind these books - to give you as much information as possible in the fewest words necessary, to get things done quicker!

> *Deductive thinkers want the point and the details that support it first, and inductive thinkers need to hear the details first before they can consider the point.*

Connection and Understanding

Most women want to explain, justify and go through the details of why a problem has occurred, whereas the majority of men just want to focus on solving the problem. If a woman takes too long to explain what the problem is, a man can lose interest and move on and not even solve the problem, while the woman is still trying to explain things. That is one of the reasons women can feel unheard. This may be a sweeping statement, so go and observe this and decide for yourself.

The number one complaint that women have in relationships is: "I don't feel heard." According to author John Gray in *Men Are from Mars, Women Are from Venus*, this isn't because she hasn't been physically heard—of course the man has heard what she has said. What the woman means is that she doesn't feel *understood*.

Sometimes I can see that people switch off as I'm going through the details of a problem; in the man's brain, he is saying to himself, "Get to the point, get to the point," which then leads to, "I'm going to switch off soon, so I'll interrupt her and I'll guess what she wants me to do so I can get on with it." Maybe the man is right and she is going on and on and on, but if he's wrong and the guess that he interrupts with isn't correct, then the frustration and confusion only intensify.

If you feel that you are not heard at work, take a step back and ask yourself, is it because no one is listening, or is it because you're not clear and concise enough in what you want to say and how you present it? If the latter is the case, what can you do differently so that they do listen intently? Think about it and reflect on a time this may have happened to you. I'm a big fan of always asking myself, "What could I have done differently to come across better? What objections did I get? Could I have explained myself better? Could I have involved them in a different way? Was I too defensive and negative?" Sometimes, when we reflect and ask questions of ourselves, we can see things differently. Doesn't it make sense why in some cases you can reflect and realise that you could have indeed done things differently to obtain a better result?

Now, don't get me wrong, there may be many situations when this is not the case; however, the way to handle these situations is exactly what we'll cover in the next chapters. Understanding the differences in how a man's brain thinks just may help in how we communicate when dealing with men. Bear in mind that this will apply to some women, too.

Another way to think about dealing with complex situations and problem-solving is the old saying from author Stephen Covey, "Seek first to understand, then to be understood." This has helped me on lots of occasions. Sometimes I used to get so focused on my own outcome that I couldn't understand why my point wasn't coming across and why those I was speaking with didn't agree with me, until I actually thought to myself, *First try to understand why and what the other person's thoughts are.* Then I was able to explain my own thoughts. It works every time.

Seek first to understand, then to be understood.

It's not about being right or wrong; it's about seeking to understand others' thoughts and objections, to understand why they think the way they do. This will help you to either change your approach or your desired outcome.

As a society, we seem to have lost the skill of listening. We spend more time listening to react rather than *really* listening to what is being said. Practise your listening skills. When you listen, it has many benefits: 1) the other person feels heard, 2) they appreciate you listening to them and they feel valued, and 3) you get to really understand them. Only then will you also be listened to in return.

I mentioned mirror and matching earlier in this chapter, and I wanted to touch on that idea again, as sometimes mirror and matching can turn out to be a negative thing. As women try to grow and develop their careers, often they look at people around them who have achieved that growth and look to copy how they did it. I did this on more than one occasion. Why did I do it? Why copy other people's behaviours and not just be myself?

Upon reflection, I think I did this because I thought that was the right way to do it, to be accepted, to fit in and to grow my career. I didn't realise at the time that it would change me. One thing to consider when looking at other people who have achieved what you want to achieve: if it is a man, then you will copy the masculine traits of his character, and that is more often than not where women can go wrong. They start to mimic the behaviour of men, to try to get into the men's club! They become too masculine in their approach, and even masculine in their language. I have even seen women, including me, change the way they dress. Some women stop being women and start becoming men in their style of communication. We all have someone we work with, have met or know that this has happened to. Don't be that person. It's not real, it's not who you really are, and this is where things start to go wrong. You don't feel yourself. You argue more, you stop enjoying your work and then it spirals away with itself. Then the job you loved no longer loves you.

Communication is about being authentic, confident, and assertive, but to do this, we need to learn how to communicate effectively. This includes communicating with women, with men, and, most importantly, with ourselves. Communication is a complex area, and we all, whether male or female, whether young or old, whether at work or home, need to understand communication better in order to have happy, fulfilling lives without fear, conflict, and frustration. Communication and confidence are learnt skills. You are not born with them. Yes, some people's characters ooze confidence, but that's because they choose to do so—and you can choose to do this too. You can choose to learn more things that make you feel confident. You can choose to communicate more effectively. So never be put off by this. You too can feel this way.

Have you noticed that here we are talking about feelings, and, in turn, we have different types of feelings, and those feelings are controlled by our thoughts? Our thoughts control our feelings, and our feelings control our actions. I hear the penny dropping, as it did with me many years ago.

The power is ours to decide on who we want to be, regardless of how others behave towards us; we are women who choose.

> *It is in your power to choose who you want to be.*

Top Tips to Remember

1. **Daily Reflection.** The way we communicate tells the world who we are. Start to reflect on how you communicate.

   Do you use email instead of picking up the phone and talking to someone?

   Write a daily journal to reflect on your day.

   Did you come across the way you wanted or were there any areas you felt you could improve?

   What were they and what could you do differently?

   Once you start reflecting and notice those things, you can see the things that need to change.

   Ask yourself if you could have communicated better. Learn and try a new approach and see how things change.

2. Practise, practise, practise. Watch your own words and how you communicate to yourself. Are you empowering yourself or limiting yourself? Communication is a critical skill, so practise it.

3. Don't forget - it's not just the words you speak, it's the thoughts you think, your tone and the speed of your voice, your body language, your attitude and your image. Most importantly, just be you. Pay attention to your body language and change it if you need to.

4. Take small steps. It is so much easier if you just start small and do things one step at a time, so notice the small things, make small changes and, when you start to see the impact, this will empower, motivate and enthuse you to do more.

Time to Reflect

Write down what you've noticed about your own communication style so far and what you're going to implement, change or learn.

_____

_____

_____

_____

_____

_____

_____

_____

_____

_____

_____

_____

_____

CHAPTER 2

— ❖ —

Men vs. Women

The Role of Gender

Over the past few years, there has been far more attention focused on gender equality than we have ever seen before, from the #MeToo campaign to International Women's Day to #choosetochallenge.

There has been an increase in regular negative posts on social media about women's perceived behaviour. Why is it that women are accused of being emotional when they feel they are just being passionate? Why is it said that women are being aggressive when they feel they're being assertive? Why do women feel that they have to "please" others and do what is expected of them instead of doing what they feel is right? Why do some female leaders get called bossy when they are leading? Why do these things come across this way? And is there any truth in these perceptions, or are they purely gender issues in the workplace? Probably both!

Many women struggle to communicate with men at work, and, of course, men will feel the same way around women for sure. *Men Are from Mars, Women Are from Venus*, the best-selling book by John Gray, demonstrates the difference in communication when looking at the interaction between men and women in relationships, but what about their interactions at work? In Gray's book, he talks about how in relationships, a woman can say something, but a man might interpret it in a completely different way, and then this is where communication goes adrift and an argument starts, even though the women didn't want to argue in the first place. But because of the words the woman used, the man becomes defensive and, of course, this goes the other way as well and can cause a reaction that was never even intended. Women can use the same words as men but express those words with a different emotional emphasis which is why misunderstandings can happen. In his book, John Gray gives a great example here;

For example, a woman may say, "We never go out."

A man may pick that up and think, "That's not true, we went out last week." And he may also hear "You're not doing your job, what a disappointment you have turned out to be, we never do anything together anymore because you are lazy, unromantic and boring". What the woman did mean is that she feels like going out and doing something together. We always have such a fun time and I love being with you, so what do you think, shall we go out this week? If she had used this statement, what a difference the man would feel and I bet his response would be exactly as she had hoped; another date night.

Now, it may be asked, why didn't the woman just tell him what she wanted and how it made her feel in the first place? That way the man can feel needed and loved. I can see my partner, Rob, rolling his eyes right now! He always talks about this and how it happens at work and, to be fair, at home too; "Just say what it is you want"! One question I hear a lot from men is, "Why don't women just say what they want?" Instead, we go all around the houses and men must try and work it out. Welcome to the world of *Men Are from Mars, Women Are from Venus*. So, grab that book. It's an inside view of how both our brains work. When you do read this book about relationships, it is definitely an eye-opener to *both* behaviours, and you can understand why miscommunication can take place. It really does explain the differences in how men and women think and how we will clash if we don't understand those differences in our loving relationships.

Men can be very direct and say exactly what they want, but most women find it hard to do that, and this is where we can lose our voices. It's important to work out for yourself why this is the case and what's holding you back. Why can't we just simply say what we want? Is it fear of trust and fear of rejection? I realised that if this is happening in relationships at home, then it must be happening in the workplace as well. Being direct doesn't mean being rude; it just means saying what you want. That's it, just say it. Improving how you communicate with others not only helps in your relationship with your partner but also with your children and other family members. Don't go all around the houses; just say what it is you want, and you will be surprised how quickly you will be understood and how soon things will start to happen.

When we communicate across genders, the number one rule is that men need to feel needed whilst women need to feel wanted. This can be quite confusing though as women start to become more independent and men feel less needed.

As society changes and women do become more independent and take on careers, the "need" for the man to provide gets less, and the man can sense it. In theory, women don't "need" a man anymore the way they used to in traditional society. Why is this? It could be biological, but it's more likely sociological. In the past, and even now, men are seen as protectors and contributors. However, now women display that they no longer need to be taken care of as they can earn their own income, buy their own house and change that light bulb. So, what can we do to help each other as these changes occur?

The simple answer, in my opinion, is that both genders need to empower each other. Men need to feel like they are still needed, so we as women need to empower men to feel this way, and, likewise, as women, we need to feel wanted, and this is where men can fulfil that role by empowering us and supporting us in our new roles as we develop in this ever-changing world.

This is a very simple way of looking at things, but it may just give you an insight and explain why relationships break down. I'm sure there is much more psychology around this, but I am all for keeping it simple so we can understand and take action easily and quickly in order to change our lives. We don't need to understand how electricity works to turn on the light; we just press the switch. Put simply, I believe both men and women still need to feel needed and wanted. I mean, who doesn't, if we're being honest? We just need to work out how we still do that as society changes.

I am using the terms "male" and "female," but this is also applicable when people are more feminine or masculine in their character traits. Their needs still need to be fulfilled. This book was originally about frustrations in communicating with men in the workplace and trying to understand why women feel overlooked, unheard and uninvolved and why this was happening. Is it a male versus female issue or just about bad communication skills, a lack of understanding, or ego? And whatever it is, what can we do to improve it? It appears to be a combination of all of these factors.

Whilst there are differences in significant dynamics between men and women and the way we communicate, as I did more and more research, the conclusion came to me that this book should also talk about how important communication is, not just with men but with other women too, as well as with ourselves. The differences in communication in how we do it and how it is received, determines our responses. This impacts our whole life. You can hopefully see how important this really is.

Whilst our world should no longer be just a man's world, some industries are more dominated by men than women, and in those industries, gender inequality can be, and still is, in the dark ages. It doesn't matter what position you hold, from office administrator to supervisor, manager, or board director, learning to work with sexual discrimination and gender equality is still a challenge. Sexism can occur not just in the boardroom but in meetings, the office, the canteen and even in the interview room.

Even after years of gender equality being high on the agenda of issues to address, some industries are still so far behind that one wonders if they will ever change, but that doesn't mean we will give up. As humans, we are social beings. We have a need to feel connected to each other; therefore, those we hang around with will influence our values and beliefs. The only way to create change in society is to create awareness, to talk about the problems, highlight them and challenge them. As society starts to change, all of these old values and beliefs need to change across generations, which is why creating change can be so slow. We need to be patient whilst this happens, but we also need to constantly challenge situations to keep things moving forward. The more we challenge, the higher the awareness becomes. The more we ask questions in the workplace, the more quickly we will see change. From challenge comes change, so let's #choosetochallenge for a better future for ourselves and for future generations.

Our Brains

There are many studies into the differences between men's brains and women's brains that contradict each other, but most studies do agree in a couple of areas.

One large-scale study by a research team at the University of Basel focused on determining the gender-dependent relationship between emotions, memory performance and brain activity. The study used a technique called FMRI, which measures and maps brain activity. It showed that 696 female participants had increased brain activity when shown negative emotional pictures. "This result would support the common belief that women are more emotionally expressive than men," explained Dr Klara Spalek, lead author of the study. Look at your own behaviour and that of those around you; I know it's always me who starts crying at the sad parts of movies or even at adverts! However, it's not just in negative situations that women cry—it can be happy ones, too. I always cry at the Christmas John Lewis advert, even if it's a happy one! In fact, I think we are now conditioned to cry at this advert before it even starts. I notice female work colleagues show more compassion than men do when another female at work needs extra support at work or with a home problem. That's not to say that men don't have the same care and compassion, but it does indicate that women are more emotionally expressive than men.

We also need to acknowledge that hormones play a part. Men's and women's hormones exist, and they provide different functions to us. Men have more testosterone and women have more progesterone and oestrogen. These are not just hormones; they are chemical transmitters and change the way we think. Our sex hormones drive different behaviours between women and men. Oestrogen will drive more maternal behaviour and testosterone will drive more territorial behaviour.

So, depending on the levels of hormones that are present in our bodies at any point in time, mixed in with conversations that clash in values and beliefs, there is no wonder that, at times, we have conflict. But again, this can be the same for both sexes communicating with each other as well as opposite sexes communicating. In summary, be aware of the way you communicate with your emotions and be aware of when your emotions are heightened. This means you need to pay even more attention to your thoughts, feelings and actions. I know we can get carried away with our emotions when we feel passionate about what we're trying to achieve.

Another important note to remember is that men can find strong women in the workplace unusual, especially since it wasn't too long ago that women stayed home to take care of their families. If a husband and father is the more dominant figure in a household, their child can grow into an adult believing that the male is always the more dominant one, the one who makes all the decisions, the one who earns the most money to look after the family, the one who disciplines and challenges the children. So, when the child grows up to be a young male adult and enters the workplace, they have grown up in a totally different environment. Should this young male adult then have a female boss, he may find it difficult to be managed by a female rather than a male. In the same way, if this male adult became a manager, you can see why he might dismiss female ideas and challenges, as he might feel that it's not their place to bring up their own suggestions. This can cause resistance to women and, potentially, discrimination. My conclusion on this topic about men vs women is quite simple; women need to be clear and direct about what they want and how they say what they want. You don't need to be rude; just be clear without the waffle and remember how a man needs to feel needed.

Here is an example of how conversations may go in a work environment. You're in a meeting with your manager talking about your review as your probationary period is about to finish and he asks you about how you are feeling about the role and if you have any concerns. Your manager is male. You have a problem with your workspace as you're using a laptop which is causing back and shoulder pain from staring at the screen. You may start the conversation by stating that you get on well with everyone in the office and you're enjoying the role. It may be that you heard money was tight in the company now and therefore you won't ask for an extra screen that you want as they can't afford it. Or you have heard that your manager has a tight budget to stick to this year, so either you don't ask or you start to say something like this; "There is one thing though, you see, erm, what I want to say is, well, it's not that important really, especially if the budget is tight and we can talk about it in a few months' time, so er, never mind, we can wait until then". Or you could be more direct and simply ask for what you want. For example, "I really enjoy working with you and the support you and the team have shown has been brilliant so thank you for that and can you help me with something else?". They will always say, "Yes, how can I help you?" You are asking for help and saying that you need them. Everyone likes to help someone and, by asking for help, the man will feel needed. You can also justify why you need their help: "Could I please have a screen to work off instead of my laptop screen? It's causing me back and shoulder pain; that would be really great if you could help me with that". Can you see the difference?

Another instance can be; "I have a deadline to meet, and I hope the suppliers deliver on time otherwise we will fail the launch date. I really do hope that they can do it as I worry that things will get pushed back further and further. Oh well, I did ask them to make sure they delivered on the date I asked for so we will have to wait and see." Sometimes, as women, we don't want to hassle someone else with our workload, so we will hint that we need help but don't actually ask for it! However, if you said it like this; "I have a deadline to meet for a project I'm working on and I could really do with your help; please could you talk to the suppliers and ask for a commitment to the delivery date of the new part that's going to be ordered? That way we can achieve the deadline with a few spare days up our sleeve in case we get delayed anywhere else. I really appreciate your help with this. Thank you."

I started to notice the difference in responses from men when I changed my words when asking for help with something; the impact was incredible. I switched from using the word 'could' to the word 'would'. The word 'could' is a word to describe an ability to do something whereas the word 'would' is a request to do something. These two words are very similar and it's hard to describe the difference between the two of them but one does appear to work more than the other. It has a more direct approach to ask someone to do something. Because of its direct, clear approach, you are more likely to get engagement from a man. I think, as women, we may use the word 'could' more often as it feels more polite and, as most women fear rejection more than men, then we would be more cautious in our approach when asking for help. However, this will not necessarily get the response that we want. Men want clear instruction and direction as to how they can help or fix a problem, therefore, a more direct style of request is likely to be the better approach.

Men can have a slightly different meaning to these words. In the book, *Men are from Mars and Women are from Venus*, this area was also explored and the author asked various men at one of his conferences about the use of the words could and would. One man describes that when a woman uses 'could', as in 'could you please help?', it sounds critical to him, like he's already failed her but if she asked 'Would you please carry this?' it sounds like an opportunity for him to be the good guy and he wants to say yes. Another man said that with the word 'would', as in 'Would you help?', he felt he had a choice and wanted to help.

Another approach to be aware of is being too critical even when you think you are being constructive. A man hates to be criticised. It makes him feel like he has failed and is not worthy. It's the worst thing a woman can do and a man feels like you are really putting him down, even where a woman may feel it's a basic request. For example, "You never put the bin out; could you do it now?" Already, you are telling him he has failed as you think he never puts the bin out and using the word 'could' makes him feel he has failed as well. Even if he does take the bin out, he'll be muttering words of discontent about you. If you had just asked what you wanted which is, "Would you take the bin out, please?", this is a clear request and he is more likely to want to do it to please you and to also feel like he is helping you. It may feel like a small change of words to you, but to a man, this is a huge difference. Most importantly, make sure you take the time out to say thank you when he does take the bins out. Thanking someone for their help is such a compliment to the other person and makes them feel proud for what they have done. When you make someone feel like that, don't you think that they will always want to help you out?

Let's talk about this in a work context. "Gary, you never take the minutes in the meeting. Could you do it now?" versus "Gary, would you take the minutes for this meeting, please?" The first approach embarrasses him in front of people, so you belittle him. He may feel he has let his team down as he hasn't taken the minutes yet and he will certainly feel pressured to do something he didn't want to do. With the second approach, it's just a clear request for help. "Would you take the minutes for this meeting, please?" There is no hidden meaning that anyone can take from it; it's a simple request that he take the minutes of the meeting. You can really feel the difference in the approach. Try it out and see how it works for you.

There are so many different examples of this and it is so fascinating to see how the use of different words and approaches when talking with the opposite sex can have a profound outcome. In my experience, the tips below can really help to improve communication with both sexes, however, when understanding how differently we both communicate with each other and the reasons behind it, these can make communication far easier and more impactful.

Top Tips to Remember

1. Remember. you can work everything out; there's always a way. When talking to a man, be clear and direct. Explain what you want and why.

2. Men always respond to praise; tell him what he does well and because he has that strong skill, you want him to help you. Men always want to be praised and appreciated and they also want to fix things and help.

3. Ask questions. Ask for feedback. Men like to feel they are giving and connecting so, by asking more questions, you get them more involved and the more someone feels involved and connected to you, the better chance you have of them working with you.

4. If you find yourself in a situation where you sense that you are being challenged or discriminated against because of being a woman, remember to take a step back, pause and think about the situation and be direct – "Are you behaving like this because I'm a woman?" or "You do know that sexism in the workplace is no longer accepted". Gosh, it does stop people in their tracks and make them think. 80% of the time, people don't realise that they are behaving in a discriminative way.

5. Switch using the word 'Could' to 'Would'.

6. Be direct in your request. Don't go all around the houses explaining why; just ask the question.

7. Remember, you are a strong confident woman, so lean in, speak up and contribute to a situation. Don't be deterred by the fact that, as women and men, our brains and hormones may make us think differently; we can still communicate to each other to get the same results we are looking for.

Time to Reflect

Write down the last time you felt awkward in conversation with a man. What was being said and how could you have reacted differently? How could that have changed the outcome? What will you do differently next time? Remember that you need to practise this too, so be patient.

CHAPTER 3

---◆◆◆---

#MeToo

The #MeToo phrase was first coined in 2006 by Tarana Burke. She is an advocate for women and is based in New York. She created the #MeToo campaign for women who had endured sexual violence, harassment or abuse. In 2017, after the exposure of Harvey Weinstein, the movement began to spread virally as a hashtag on social media. American actress Alyssa Milano posted on Twitter, "If all the women who have been sexually harassed or assaulted wrote '~me too' as a status, we might give people a sense of the magnitude of the problem." Calling out #MeToo helps to bring awareness that sexual harassment still does go on.

Discrimination of any kind should not be tolerated at work and in society, and hopefully, if you are experiencing any kind of discrimination, this book will help you. The key is to ensure that we can communicate effectively should we come across sexism in the workplace and make sure that we are equipped and have the tools to manage any signs of potential harassment with a clear, confident voice.

Life is far better for women today than it used to be. We get more opportunities and more support than ever, but it can *still* be tough. Even today, where it is no longer "meant" to be a man's world, it certainly is in many industries. Even after years of being in your position, and even when you do make it to the boardroom, there are still day-to-day sexist comments, actions and behaviours to deal with. There are some so-called jokes, which can be funny when they are just about the differences between a man and a woman, as let's not forget, there are jokes about men too. However, sometimes they just go too far and we need to know when to draw the line, know what to do and say and respect one another. In the next few chapters, we talk about this and the best way to handle unwanted comments and behaviours.

I also want to make it clear that communication problems are not just about feminism and women's rights. If we're not careful, we will go too far the other way. I like being treated with respect. I want to be called an author, an entrepreneur, a leader or a founder. Why do I have to be a female leader, a female founder or a female entrepreneur? I like it when a man or a woman opens the door for me, and I love receiving compliments; I mean, who doesn't? I also like to hold the door open for a man or a woman; it's simply good manners and respect. I love to hear a wolf whistle or be told I'm wearing a nice jacket or dress, but some women don't, so how do men deal with that? Do they stop communicating with us in fear of our reaction?

It's vitally important to remember that we need to help men understand what we want and not simply tell them what we *don't* want and end up pushing them away. If we're not careful, women could end up being accused of gender inequality themselves in some circumstances!

I've heard some really disturbing stories that women have faced at work and it makes my blood boil; I wonder why they didn't speak up, but until you are faced with a situation, you never know how you will react.

When I was Managing Director, I had to attend various networking events both here in the UK and overseas. I remember being at one event with a male colleague and every single time someone spoke to us, they introduced themselves to him first and spoke at length before they even turned to me for an introduction. I guess you could say that was bad manners and not necessarily ignoring me as a female. On one occasion, when my colleague introduced me to a man as his boss, his reaction was "Oh God, how do you cope with that as your boss?" I was stunned that he referred to me as 'that'! After what seemed like the slowest 10 seconds of my life as I pondered on how to respond, I also thought, 'I am not allowing you to get away with it' so I said, "Excuse me, now that's not very polite, is it?" He fumbled with his words and apologised that he didn't mean any offence and we carried on our conversation. I was also quite shocked at how direct men can be when it comes to asking certain questions. Once, another Managing Director, who was at the as level as me, turned to me at a meeting and asked me how long I had been sleeping with the boss! Another winked at me and said, "It's alright for you women, you just sleep your way to the top and now that the government want to look at forcing companies to put women on boards, us men will have no chance"! The one thing I do on every single occasion is call out these men. I responded to both of them by saying, "Now, don't be insecure; you focus on your job, and I'll focus on mine," and simply moved on. Now, at first, I didn't say a word at all as I was so shocked and embarrassed and speechless that I didn't know what to say, but I'll be damned if they were going to try and intimidate me, or stop my focus, determination and passion for my job and my continued success would prove otherwise to them. There have been too many occasions where I have been at an event and my male partner has been assumed to be the one working in the industry and I was, as one man put it, either his wife or his work lover! It still infuriates me to this day; you never get used to it.

I think my point is this; if we want change, then we must call them out. I've watched and read various stories of the terrible abuse that

Hollywood and the acting and movie industry has endured, and I have always wondered why some of these women just didn't and don't say no and walk away. When they were asked to do certain things so they could get a role or a promotion, why did they do it and not simply just say no? We are taught and we teach in schools that no means no, so why did they say yes? To secure that job, that role? If some did say yes to get what they wanted, it's not right to call the person out later. Joan Collins talks about this and how Marilyn Monroe warned her about how Hollywood was so different to the British movie industry and the terrible abuse that took place. She warned Joan about what would be expected of her and Joan decided to say no and would not be used in that way. Her career took longer to take off but she still stood up and said no and still had successful movie and TV roles and, more to the point, she had a long-standing career. We all have a choice. Now, please don't misunderstand me; there are many different circumstances and situations where fear and threatening mentally abusive behaviour has been used against women where they didn't think that they had a choice. This is exactly why I have written this book so that women can understand that no matter what the situation you are in, you do have a choice and you can change your circumstances and we are all here to help and support you to make that happen. There are so many support groups to reach out to that will help change your circumstances no matter how tough they may seem. There is always a way.

However, as a client once said to me, "But I'm not as strong and as tough as you and wouldn't dare stand up". This is why, as women, we have to support each other, learn the skills to be more confident and push through our own insecurities. Understand that what we may have been taught growing up is simply wrong and, in today's society, we do have a choice.

Sometimes, it is not as simple as I have just described but we do have a choice. I do apologise if you think it's repetitive to keep using this phrase over and over again in this book, but I want you to always remember this - you do have a choice. I remember learning about how our choices determine our future. There was a study done once of two brothers who had an abusive drunk father who was in and out of prison all his life. When the two brothers were grown up, they were interviewed about their life. One of them was a drunk and in and out of prison and the other was a successful lawyer. They were both asked a question; "Why has your life turned out the way it has?" and they both said exactly the same thing; "What do you expect with a father like that?!" One said, "There was no way I was going to allow my life to turn out the way he has; I wanted more from life. I wanted self-respect, to be healthy and have a loving family so I had to do the opposite of what my own father did, and each day, I'm so glad I chose to do that." The other son said, "I'm just like my dad, so what do you expect?" So, you can see how our circumstances and events that happen to us do not determine our future; our decisions do.

Once, whilst in America on a training course. I met a truly incredible young woman. She was 28 years old, living in South America where she was working full time and also volunteered her time to help female victims of domestic abuse. She grew up in a village where she was continually beaten and repeatedly raped by members of her own family and the community. She worked every day doing whatever jobs she could to find the money to save up for a bus fare. As soon as she had enough, at 16 years old, she ran away from her family to be rid of the abuse once and for all. In her mind, she said, 'I will not be a victim. I couldn't physically fight back and say no as they just beat me, so I had to find another way to end the nightmare I was living in. I have a choice,' she said to herself, 'and I choose to survive and I will choose my own life'. She told herself, each and every day, 'I'm strong and I will survive'; it was her affirmation and her strength of mind that got her through. It was a choice. Her story will stay with me forever. I could write another book on fabulous stories like this of strength, courage and determination. There are so many, and whilst this is an extreme set of circumstances, some abuse does take place in normal everyday environments that we simply don't expect.

I recently heard a story that showed how our conditioning as we grow up affects the way we, as women, can react; even when we know something is seriously wrong, we don't speak up. It's very easy to judge the story I'm about to tell you as, if I am being honest, I did too. I had a conversation with a friend who was at an event that her husband was attending for his work. She knew most of the people there and had done so for years. It was an evening event and dinner was being served with wine which was flowing freely. As the lady stood at the bar, a man she knew was telling her how great her husband was and all that he was doing with his life. As he went to walk away, he said, "Just a cheeky squeeze of the breast," and he did just that and walked off!! She was frozen, speechless, and just stood there in shock. She said many thoughts went through her mind. "Oh my god, did he really just do that? What should I do? How dare he! Do I scream and shout at him?" She replied to herself, "No, don't do that. It's my husband's work; don't embarrass him and it will cause a scene"! Note that she has said 'It will cause a scene, don't embarrass him', meaning her husband. What the hell? Who cares about that?! When she told me, I was fuming! How dare he violate her like this? Why did he think he had the right to touch her and why didn't she call him out? When I asked her about this, she said it was something that her parents had said to her as a child - "Don't cause a scene", and that was it, so she didn't! She decided not to say anything to anyone and would tell her husband at home when it was all over. I sat there and couldn't believe it. Why did she not speak up there and then? Why did she let him get away with it? He could do this to another woman, so why would you let that happen? I took a deep breath and thought about what I would have done. I reckon I would have grabbed his hand and shouted at the top of my voice that he was not to touch me. But yes, there would have been a scene and I knew my partner Rob would then probably have a go at the chap and there would be more trouble, but there is no way I would allow him to do that and walk off. Or would I? Do we really know how we would react if something like this happened to us? We think we do but until it does, would we? Would fear freeze us and then the moment passes, and we walk away? What would we do?

I hope that this book helps to give you the confidence that if this ever did happen to you, you would kick him in the balls and bring him to his knees!!!!! Seriously, I don't mean that, but what I do want and hope for is that if this did ever happen to me or any one of you, you would say, "Stop! That is unacceptable and do not touch me again", and, depending on the circumstances, report him. I am sure there are many stories out there like this, so the key is to ensure we build up our own confidence that it won't happen in the first place, and then, in the second place, to know what to do if it did. This client did tell her husband the next day and he did deal with the situation. As we don't know all the circumstances and we can't predict people's reactions, we don't know if it was the right thing to do to wait to confront the situation the following day when no alcohol was involved and the conversation could take place in a better, more productive way.

When the #MeToo campaign came out and there were so many accusations that followed, it proved that by speaking out, it gives other women the courage to do it too.

As women, we also need to understand men's thoughts and points of view. A man I once coached showed concerns that he no longer knew how to communicate with women in fear of offending them after all the publicity of the #MeToo campaign. He asked, "If I compliment a woman on her clothing, will I be accused of harassment? If I talk to her for too long about things other than work, will I be seen to be flirting?"

"Of course not," I answered. "Just make sure you read that the other person wants you to engage in those types of conversations. You will be able to tell through her reactions, her responses and her body language. And most of all, be respectful and be kind." So, it's critical that whilst we ensure women are taken seriously and make it clear that certain behaviours are unacceptable, we must include men when trying to create change. Tell them what is acceptable to you and what isn't. I am quite a touchy-feely person and I'm used to working with other cultures where they greet by kissing each other on the cheek. However, I know women who do not like to be hugged, kissed or touched in any shape or form so we need to express what we do want and what we don't, otherwise, how the heck will the man know?

The whole theme should be about inclusion, not exclusion, working together and not against gender diversity, and supporting each other to make change happen—and, more importantly, to make it happen permanently. However, I must strongly add that, at times, women do cling to the gender issue, and sometimes you just need to get over it, toughen up and focus on what you want, not just on the problem. Our society and culture will not change overnight so don't be too sensitive over some things. Sometimes, we do need to toughen up, speak out to change our society. When you portray this intent of inclusion and this strong focus on what you want, you will be amazed by how others will change their behaviours towards you.

Many women I know ask me why I have never had any issues with being a woman in the workplace, and I answer, "Quite frankly, I will simply not allow it. I know what I want, I focus on it, and this gives strong energy and a strong persona. I think it scares anyone off who might give me issues!" Now, that's not to say I haven't had or don't have my own inner insecurities about speaking up, as I certainly do have those insecurities, but more on that later. I remember one time having a meeting booked with a customer and we were due to hold it in a hotel reception where a lot of other people have coffee and hold business meetings. We were due to meet at 5:30 pm. When I was driving to meet him, I thought to myself, 'Why are we meeting here at this hotel when his office is just around the corner, and why so late in the day too?' As I sat staring at the red light at the traffic lights, my gut started to churn. 'Hold up, what if we're meeting here because he wants something else? No, I thought I would be able to tell if he was flirting with me, but then again, why are we not meeting in his office?' My head and my gut were now telling me to cancel and re-arrange the meeting. So, I called him up and told him that I was ever so sorry but needed to cancel the meeting. He responded with "That's a shame as I booked a room for us". What the hell?! Why did I not see that coming? So, yes, trust your gut instinct and listen to your thoughts. I did meet him again at his office and, for the first two meetings after, I took my boss too, just in case!

The challenge in the workplace is to allow women the same rights as men for equal pay and benefits at work. Promotion to the boardroom is still a far cry from being open, fair and equal.

It's more important than ever to know your value, speak up and learn the tools that will support you at work and in your career. Cultural change doesn't happen overnight, as we've seen with many other societal issues, so we must keep challenging ourselves to keep moving forward and never give up.

A word of warning. Please do not be the woman who uses her female assets in the thought that this will get you what you want. Yes, women do it and you can see it a mile away. You don't need to do that to be successful at work. You don't need to use your female assets to succeed, and those women who do, sadly, give the rest of us a reputation that we don't want. And, in the end, more importantly, they never usually get what they really want for the long term anyway.

We want to be happy at work, we want to succeed at work with our own skills, our own drive and our own determination and we don't want to feel used, abused and violated in doing so. If you feel you have to use your female assets, I would suggest you look at why you feel you need to. Do you not have the skills required to do the job? If this is the case, get more training. Get a clear career path mapped out and plot how you will get what you want; lay out your plan. Or does this go deeper? Is it because of other personal insecurities? Maybe there were circumstances that you have experienced that showed you this was the way to get attention and you had experienced the results by doing so.

Start reflecting on why you would want to do this instead of focusing on your own skillset to succeed. Most of the time, it's due to a lack of confidence in your own ability to do the role and this is a second option. However, you do have more options, better choices and a whole load of support, training and other experienced women who will encourage you to make better choices.

There are many groups you can connect with on social media that give you support, advice and tips. Some people set them up to make a point about being female, such as 'The Female Entrepreneur' or the 'Female Leader', or 'Female Founder', whilst the use of gender in the titles shows women that they can do it too. Some women do question why the female gender should be in the title in the first place and that they don't need any special attention just because they are female. For me, just get on and do it. Don't sweat the small stuff; just use your common sense, focus on what you want and ignore the rest; it's only noise and distraction. Years ago, when I was a Managing Director, I remember being interviewed for the

Yorkshire Post over my opinion of the UK government having targets for women to be on boards. I disagreed with the UK Government making it target-driven as women want to be awarded the position because of their talent, hard work and skill and not just because she's a woman/female and it ticks a box. We also don't want men to think we got the position just to hit a target either. However, if we don't encourage targets, how will we ever change things when the gender bias goes on unconsciously? It does raise awareness and it does make businesses, industries, and people reconsider their views and opinions - are they fair, open and equal and do they reflect internally?

Top Tips to Remember

1. Discrimination of any kind is not acceptable and, in most areas, is illegal.

2. Talk to someone about any worries or concerns no matter how small. Even if you are in doubt about whether someone, or some situation, making you feel like you are being discriminated against is really discrimination, talk it through with either a close friend or work colleague or seek professional help. There are resources for doing so at the end of this book.

3. The most important part is to finish this book. The only reason that discrimination occurs is usually from the insecurities of the other person. It's like dealing with a bully. The minute you show your confidence and assertiveness in a voice with courage and strength, the other person will recognise their inappropriate behaviour and more than likely apologise and correct themselves. Indeed, they will definitely know that YOU will not accept the inappropriate behaviour and will stop. The way you do this is through communication. The remainder of this book will show you how.

4. Seek the support of your HR Team. Have confidence that they will guide you and support you in this area; it is their role to protect you. By talking to them, it doesn't mean they will necessarily take immediate action; it may be that they will guide and help you speak up about what is acceptable and what isn't. Many people have told me that they wouldn't speak to the HR Manager in fear of the problem turning back onto themselves, but this would never be the case. They will help you.

5. Seek the support of groups on social media. Your industry may have its own network groups such as women in manufacturing, women in

law, women in defence, women in logistics. There are many groups out there so never feel alone.

6. If you are experiencing unwanted attention of any sort, no matter what, say no and seek help.

Time to Reflect

Write down what you've noticed about your own communication style so far and what you're going to implement, change or learn.

_____

_____

_____

_____

_____

_____

_____

_____

_____

_____

_____

_____

_____

CHAPTER 4

—◆—

Choose to Be in Control—Be Passionate, Not Emotional

It seems that when women become passionate, we are accused of being "emotional." One thing is for certain: when a man says to a woman, "You're getting emotional," it makes her feel ten times worse, and the emotion that is being felt at the time gets more and more intense. Before you know it, World War III has just started. Sound familiar?

But you never seem to hear the same thing being said to a man: "You're getting emotional." Why is that?

I personally think that women's brains are more emotionally connected to everything we do and men's brains are more practical than emotional, but I'm not a neuroscientist, just a life observer! It doesn't really take much to work it out, though.

Women naturally show and convey their feelings with greater emotional expressivity than men, hence the reason men comment on it. As women, we seem to react more to our own emotions than men do, and maybe that's why we're called emotional more frequently.

So, the question has to be, how do we control our emotions whilst still being passionate about the work we do? We don't want to stop being passionate, after all; we just need to be aware of our emotions and how we keep them in check.

Our passionate moments can become emotional not just at work but in our home lives too, so it's even more important for us to try to understand what makes us shift from being passionate to getting emotional. You may wonder, can you be emotional and passionate at the same time? I believe you can, but you must learn how to control your emotions so they don't run away with themselves, and of course, you must express the right ones at the appropriate times.

In the workplace, it is true to say that passion is received in a positive light and emotion has a negative connotation around it, so it's critical to know how to ensure you communicate in a positive way to get your message across.

Usually, we start off being passionate and then, through frustration, this is where our message can turn emotional. This tends to occur when you feel like no one is listening to you or like someone is disagreeing with your point of view or talking over you in a conversation that you are passionate about. How many times has this happened to you? For me, it's been way too many, I can tell you! I wish I had learnt more about communication years ago, and maybe my journey through my career may have been more enjoyable instead of feeling like a battle.

I remember visiting a customer whose business I had tried to win for years. It was so frustrating that I couldn't get a foot in the door. To be fair to my competitors, they had good service, good quality and a strong, competitive price. The only way to get the business was to buy, and that only meant one thing: lost margin. There was no way we were going to be busy fools by doing it, so I thought I would just wait, stay in contact and give the customer invaluable information on market performance and future innovation plans each month in the hopes that I would stay on their radar in case they had any issues, to be at the forefront of their minds for the next round of negotiations.

One day, I received a phone call. It was music to my ears. The customer had an issue with their delivery and asked if I could help them out. "Of course," I said, rather too quickly, as my enthusiasm showed instantly at their misfortune of a failed delivery. I took the details and called in the order. It was planned for three days' time, so there was plenty of time to arrange production and transport. The customer was thrilled to keep his factory going; otherwise, he would have had downtime for three days, which would have resulted in wages to pay for no work, fines from his customer for failed deliveries and the risk of losing his own customer. We had saved the day, or so I thought.

The following day, I received a phone call to say that there had been a power cut in our factory, so no product was going to be made that day, but we could still meet the delivery time, as we had the time to make the product the day after. I did wonder why the power cut would make a difference, as we should have had stock, but apparently, the stock count had been wrong the week before and we had nothing left, and we hadn't made any extra at the start of the week, either. I did wonder to myself why the heck we were so disorganised. If they were better organised, they would be prepared for any power cut, and they wouldn't have the issues, I moaned to myself.

Then, later that day, I received another phone call from a colleague from the transport department, who was complaining that they couldn't get a booking-in time for the delivery. The customer had now closed for the day.

My immediate thoughts were, why are they calling at the end of the day to get a booking slot? Why are they so unorganised? And why didn't they call yesterday for a booking slot, or even this morning? That's when

I allowed my emotions to start running away and get out of control. I started to feel frustrated, angry and overwhelmed, and the more I thought like this, the worse it got. My thoughts were driving my emotions and magnifying the situation, making me feel more and more frustrated. Instead of looking at how we could solve the problem, I started to ask why, why, why ... and how do you think that made the other person react from the transport department?

I was having a go at him, and some could say rightly so, but then, what I didn't realise was that the previous day, he had been at the hospital with his mother who had collapsed. Everything had stopped whilst he dashed to the hospital, and we had had no cover, as the other admin assistant was on holiday. The mother was fine, thank goodness.

If I had stopped and controlled my emotions, maybe I would have asked better questions, such as, "What are our options and how can I help?" This question immediately takes all emotion and frustration out of the situation and offers help and support. It turned out that this person had found two options, and he was calling for my advice as to which one we should choose. By the time I realised this, my heart was racing from frustration and I was blushing with feelings of shame for not being patient enough to allow this person the time to give me all the information and guilt from being, quite frankly, rude and jumping to conclusions! If only I had controlled my emotions, I could have reacted differently. The other person would have felt supported, and the outcome would have been the same.

The customer did end up getting their order on time and in full. The reaction from the transport man when he came off the phone: "Gosh, she got emotional over that." Well, I guess his language may have been somewhat stronger, but I think you get my point.

> *Be aware of the way you communicate with your emotions, and be aware of when your emotions are heightened, which means you need to pay even more attention to your thoughts, feelings and actions.*

Passion and emotion are strongly linked by energy. Laura Joan Katen, author of *The Communication Habit,* describes this perfectly. She says being passionate can be perceived differently depending on the audience as well as the way and degree to which you deliver that passion.

If the receivers don't share the same level of interest, they may be turned off by your passion and mislabel the positive display of energy as over-reactive and pushy. Katen concludes that when the energy behind the passion is focused and directed, it is perceived in a positive light, but when the energy lacks focus, it is interpreted as emotional. So how do we keep being passionate and not get too emotional?

Make sure you have all the information you need to express your idea or point of view. Back it up with facts and figures, and don't just give your opinion; make sure you ask for feedback on other people's thoughts and opinions so that you include them rather than being interrupted by them because you haven't considered their opinions. Asking for their participation usually helps to stop the interrupters, and you make your audience feel valued, involved and connected. Make sure you have a plan.

What's your goal, what's your action plan, and why will it work?

What areas of your presentation do you think people may disagree with? Role-play it out in your mind or with someone. What might people say and how will you respond?

If people disagree, let them; watch your feelings here and don't get defensive, as this can lean towards starting to get emotional. You'll notice if you are getting emotional about being challenged, as your heart will start to race and you may get a red flush or start to speak more quickly and stumble over your words.

Watch out for this, and if you do feel any of these feelings, then stop and breathe for a second to slow that heart down again and instead, get curious, accept the challenge and ask those you're speaking with why they disagree. Try to find an alignment where you can figure out a solution that suits both parties. You never know, the challenge may have merit, so be prepared to discuss it and talk through all the possibilities.

Some women can express themselves perfectly and stay calm and in control, whereas other women tend to bottle it all up until one day, there's an outburst of built-up frustration, and that's what can be perceived by others as being emotional.

We allow things to build up because we do not communicate early enough. Those awkward conversations are not being had, so we allow things to fester rather than facing them full-on. We have to take ownership that it is our responsibility to be able to find a way to express ourselves to get our points heard. Our emotions can either help us or hinder us. That's something to watch out for, especially when we are under stress.

There was a period where I was coaching ten different women from all different backgrounds, and they were *all* on some sort of medication. This was due to problems with stress at work, and it was all around not being able to communicate in some shape or form, and therefore, feeling frustration.

It made me emotionally frustrated and even angry that nothing was being done to help these women except prescribing them drugs. NHS doctors have no time these days to talk to patients to find out the root cause of the problems that are causing their stress in the first place and to help them seek guidance on how to resolve those problems. Most of the time, anxiety starts when we worry about a certain thing like work, money or relationships. Our thoughts cause the worry to intensify, which is how worry turns to anxiety which turns to panic attacks. It all starts with our thoughts, and, in a lot of cases, we don't need medication to solve the problem; we need to understand the cause of that problem. I don't mean that it's a doctor's job to solve these problems, but it should be their job to guide people and help find a solution instead of just prescribing drugs. Hence my passion for helping women to succeed in their work lives and their home lives.

Prescribing a drug for an issue does not solve the problem, and this has to end; otherwise, the UK will end up like the United States, where, according to a report by the National Centre for Health Statistics (NCHS), the rate of antidepressant usage among teens and adults (people ages twelve and older) increased by almost 400% during the years 1988–1994 and 2005–2008. It's becoming a trend to be on antidepressants. However, there are circumstances where medication is the only way to help someone move forward, and that I understand, but my point here is about over-prescribing when it's not really necessary.

The good news around this though is that women are two-and-a-half times more likely to be taking antidepressants than men and this statistic is probably a good thing, as it shows women are reaching out for help and could explain why suicides are higher in men than women. I do not believe that medication is reducing suicides in women; I believe that women do talk about their problems more than men do. This also reaffirms the study from earlier in the chapter that women are more emotionally responsive, and this is more likely to drive their behaviour to seek out help. My concern is that we don't need to take drugs to help ourselves.

In 2016, according to the most recent global data available from the World Health Organization (WHO), there were an estimated 793,000 suicide deaths worldwide. More than 80% were men. This is why it is so important and critical to understand our thoughts and to learn how we can control them. It also highlights the fact that we must support men in terms of their mental health and seek out the support they need in order to reduce ever-increasing statistics. The point here is that you can seek help without the prescription drugs that some people stay on for a lifetime. The only people who benefit from that are the shareholders of the pharmaceutical companies!

So, whilst women may be accused of getting emotional, it's not inherently a bad thing, as we are expressing ourselves. We must learn to direct our emotions to become controlled though, and we must choose positive emotions over negative emotions. This can be done without losing passion for your subject.

While right now we are exploring how we communicate with men, this will more than likely help our communication skills with whoever we talk to, male or female. Whilst this book is about gender differences, it's also about good communication skills—full stop. There is so much we can talk about when it comes to emotions, stress, anxiety and depression, what causes those things, and how we can deal with them. I think that will be the subject of my next book, soon to be released.

What is important is to understand how powerful our emotions are and how they affect our communication. It's also important to understand that when we don't communicate, we make things worse and allow things to build up, as mentioned earlier, when we could just be dealing with them.

Passion can be an intense emotion, strong feeling or desire that you associate with a subject, and passions are almost always associated with positive energy. Our emotions, though, can be either positive or negative, and when negative, they can get out of control. When a feeling starts to become more emotional, it can impact your thinking and, therefore, your reactions and actions. I think it's possible to be passionate and emotional about a subject at the same time, but the main problem is when your emotions become stronger and you start to express them more passionately. Now, are you confused? I was certainly confused the first time someone told me I was being "emotional"! How dare they? When someone accuses you of being emotional, it's usually associated with a negative emotion, like being upset, frustrated or even angry. For example, I can be passionate about saving the planet *and* emotional about it, as it can upset me when I see the damage we have done and continue to do. I can also be passionate about salsa dancing and be emotional *with happiness* if I watch a ballet performance.

So, my interpretation of the difference is that once I become emotional at work, it is usually due to having my beliefs challenged. For example, ensuring health and safety is strictly adhered to is non-negotiable to me, and I can get passionate about it, but once I start being upset or angry about it, that's being emotional. Being emotional displays a loss of control in how we really want to express ourselves.

I was once told by an old boss that there is only one thing you are truly in control of in life and in business, and that's your emotions. When you really think about this, it's true. Epictetus was quoted as saying, "It's not what happens to you, but how you react to it that matters." If you sense that someone is deliberately wanting to wind you up, are you going to react to it, or are you going to control your feelings and emotions and choose what you want the best outcome to be and then act accordingly?

How do you really come across when things get heated in the office or in meetings? I can reflect back on certain situations at the start of my career and cringe about how I used to respond. Instead of picking up the phone and talking, everyone seems to email, and then someone will read your email in the wrong context and take it the wrong way and react accordingly. This just makes things ten times worse and more difficult to deal with.

We are human beings and human beings are emotional, and some people feel and show their emotions more than others; the key is to control them.

> *Our emotions can either help us or hinder us. That's something to watch out for, especially when we are under stress*

In a work environment, it is likely that the most common emotions to show up will be frustration, anger and upset. At work, people usually get emotional with other colleagues rather than with projects or difficult tasks. This usually happens when someone is criticised or feels unheard.

A survey done by Totaljobs in January 2020 showed that one in three emotional events at work is triggered by colleagues. The question now is how to control our reactions and our emotions. Whilst every circumstance is different, the way to control our reactions and emotions is the same regardless of circumstances.

> *There is only one thing in life you are in control of, and that's your emotions.*

How to Control Our Emotions

Many people think they're not in control of their emotions, but you can control every single emotion. You just have to understand how. Tony Robbins, who has been a major influence in my life, taught me this many years ago. I truly believe everything he teaches should be on the school curriculum, as it is a set of basic life skills: how to control our emotions, how to know what we want and how to go and get it. His books have supported me through times of challenge as I dealt with the unknown, and they have helped me get what I wanted out of life. He has also taught me how to manage the most painful times in my life. He's the ultimate teacher of life skills and business strategy.

The number one thing that Tony Robbins has taught me is that we can change the way we feel in a heartbeat, that everything we do and feel is because of our own state of mind. Change your state, change your life. The state you are in controls everything. So, what is your state? "State of mind" is defined as the quality of one's consciousness as it relates to the outside world, as well as the perception of one's inner thoughts and emotions. According to Tony Robbins, when you're in control of your state of mind, you're the master of your emotions, and you understand that life is happening for you, not to you.

Our emotions send us messages. They are here to help us. When you feel a negative emotion, it puts your mind in an unresourceful state, so much so that you can overthink the situation, dramatise it and make it a whole lot worse than it really is. When these negative emotions creep in, they are usually fear, hurt, anger, frustration, disappointment, guilt, inadequacy, rejection, overwhelm or even loneliness. All emotions have rules attached to them—your rules. So, check in with those rules and make sure they make sense to you.

For example, did you need to feel rejected because someone interrupted you during your presentation, or did they just not understand a point that you needed to explain differently? Do you have to be defensive when someone has a different opinion or should you listen first, seek to understand them and *then* seek for yourself to be understood?

When these negative emotions come up, the key is to recognise the message and then decide if you need to change your perception and your rules around it or change your behaviours/actions. When you think of it this way, it makes it so much easier to understand and, more importantly, deal with.

It fascinates me how men can have a conflict at work and sometimes get quite angry about a subject (Oh, note how I used the word "angry" to describe how the man feels instead of "emotional"—now that is interesting), and then later that day, they can be in the pub after work, laughing over a drink.

If that were a woman, we would be seething about the situation and stewing over it all night. Why? I have no idea, but from conversations and interviews with many men and women, I have found that women do tend to take things more personally than men do.

A man once said when preparing for a difficult and awkward meeting with a supplier, "Now remember everyone, this isn't a personal thing with Derek; it's a debate over the problem we are facing, not with the argument with Derek. Let's focus on the solution and not the person."

Wow. Straight away, you could see how that meeting was going to pan out. It could so easily have focused purely on the individual and the supplier, and the language used could easily have been received as a personal attack. Focusing on finding a solution instantly made the meeting so much more constructive. Yes, it did end well, and the problems were resolved.

Top Tips to Remember

1. **Trigger Points.** Identify when you feel that you are becoming emotional. What is the trigger point and what does it mean? When you understand your trigger points, you can then know how to handle and control them. This takes time and practice, but the results that you will feel will be priceless. You will feel more confident and in control of not just yourself, but the whole situation.

2. Pause for ten seconds and check in with yourself. Seek clarity if something appears to have been misunderstood by colleagues, or indeed, by yourself. Are you being factual?

3. Get curious with your audience and ask questions.

4. Remember your facts and repeat them in a different way.

5. Check your body language, as this is just as important as the spoken word. Are you frowning or smiling? Where are your hands, on your hips? How are you standing or sitting? Are you giving out positive vibes or negative? Check the other person's body language too. People's faces and their expressions can give you a really clear indication of what they are feeling. If they are frowning, they may be confused about what you have just said, so ask them; "I can see you look confused or have a question. Would you like to explore something further about what I have just said?"

6. *Do not react.* Seek to understand first. Don't listen to reply, listen to understand their point of view. First, seek to understand to then be understood. You can always tell when someone is going to start to push your buttons; watch out for this, too. Pause and think about how you can regain control of the conversation. The easiest way to do that is to focus and direct the conversation away from your own trigger points and onto something else. If you are coming from a place to do

good, deliver more, solve a problem or improve a situation, then bring the conversation back to the subject.

7. If someone says, "I simply do not agree with what you have just said," ask them why and ask for examples of what they mean so you can respond. This is not just about how *you* respond; it's about making the other person feel involved and feel that their opinion is important—not necessarily right, but important, too.

Time to Reflect

Write down the last time you felt your emotions taking over a situation. What's the first thing you notice and remember that triggered them? What was being said and how could you have reacted differently? How could that have changed the outcome? What will you do differently next time? Remember that you need to practise this too, so be patient.

_____

_____

_____

_____

_____

_____

_____

_____

_____

_____

_____

CHAPTER 5

Learn How to Give the Right Impression—Be Assertive, Not Aggressive

How many times have women been accused of being aggressive when they are trying to be assertive? I believe that men in particular use the term "aggressive" when they come across a woman who is confident and knows what she wants to say or do and they feel threatened by it. They don't know how to respond. As mentioned earlier, if they are not used to having a strong woman in their families, it can be quite daunting to them.

My experience when this has happened to me is that telling you that you are being aggressive is a way to shut you up. The other person doesn't like what you are saying, and this is such an easy way to stop you in your tracks. I can remember a few occasions when this was said to me, and by gosh, when it was, it made my feelings of not being heard rise even higher. I'd also feel embarrassed and ashamed as I started to wonder if I was being too aggressive.

I have learned that the best approach when this situation arises is to stop talking, pause, reflect on what I have just said or done and evaluate if I am indeed being too aggressive in my approach. There are times when we do need to reflect and question if we are being too aggressive in our communication style or if we are being strong and confident.

One of the key takeaways in this book is to learn to not only challenge others but to reflect upon our own behaviours, be honest and ask ourselves if we could have handled things better.

In the past, I have associated aggression with people raising their voices, being physically threatening and making me fear what they might do. However, this may not always be the case, as aggression can and does include language as well. You might not think you are being aggressive, while the other person may feel that you are. You can then be accused of being hostile and negative and causing even more problems.

People can mix up aggressiveness and assertiveness, as they simply don't understand the meaning of each one. No one wants to be accused of being aggressive, and when we are, this escalated the situation even more, and when someone knows which buttons to press, they will indeed press them. When this happens, you can become frustrated and then lose control of what you wanted to say in the first place; being assertive is not only about words but about behaviours too.

> *Reflect on your own behaviour and language, but don't be afraid to be confident and express what you want just because it threatens someone else.*

Do not let your assertiveness and confidence diminish just because someone doesn't like them. I was once told about a situation where a woman was told that a team member she managed was accusing her of being too aggressive. The facts were that the manager had asked for a report to be done, and the timeline for submission was two weeks. Knowing that the colleague was always late in submitting her work, a week after assigning the report, the manager asked the colleague if everything was OK and checked if she needed any help to make sure that the report would be done on time. The answer was yes.

Three days before submission, the manager checked in with her colleague again to make sure everything was OK, and the answer was yes again. One day before the report was due, this person went to her manager's boss to complain that the manager was being aggressive in making sure she would have the report ready on time. The colleague couldn't understand what her problem was! The manager told her that she was just checking to make sure the report was submitted on time, as it was critical to the business. This isn't a major story, but it shows how other people can either a) be sensitive to the words and approach you use, b) need additional support but be afraid to admit it or ask, or c) use the other person's assertiveness as an excuse to justify why they are not able to achieve the outcome they agreed to. Now, there could be many different views and perceptions of this story, but the outcome is still the same: the manager was being accused of being aggressive when she felt she was being assertive in asking for what she wanted on the timeline she needed, and it was a woman accusing her of being aggressive—so this isn't just a male thing!

Not to drift on to tips on how to manage people, but it would be important for that manager to reflect on why her colleague felt this way and if she could have handled the situation any differently. We need to manage ourselves. It became clear that the colleague could not and did not want to do that particular job, and she subsequently moved on to a completely different role that suited her skill set better. In the meantime, the manager was labelled as being aggressive.

If only the colleague had spoken up to say that she didn't like her role and wanted to change it rather than shifting the focus to blame her manager for being too aggressive! Again, there are a few different approaches we could discuss here, but the point is about being aware of why we are called "aggressive" and reflecting on whether we really are, or if there is an underlying issue that needs to be addressed. The only way to know this is to ask better questions, and then the answer will show itself, as indeed it did in this case.

Whats the difference between being assertive and being aggressive?

Being aggressive is being angry and behaving in a threatening way, ready to attack. Someone who is aggressive puts others down and is disrespectful and comes across negatively. Put another way, aggression is taking charge to attack with disregard for the other party.

Being assertive is expressing opinions or desires strongly, and being self-assured with confidence. Assertiveness presents positively and respectfully.

We usually start out being assertive, and then, when the message that is being delivered isn't being received or the response isn't what we want, when we defend the position, if it's not conducted in a positive manner, the behaviour can appear aggressive.

However, I am willing to bet that when a woman is accused of being aggressive, she is highly unlikely to actually be talking in a threatening way or getting ready to attack! The likelihood is that she is being confident, direct and willing to stand up for herself, and in most cases, depending on who is in the room, it's usually the men who make the statement that a woman is being aggressive; rarely would it be other women.

> *Being assertive is expressing opinions or desires strongly, and being self-assured with confidence. It presents positively and respectfully.*

I think this is a generational problem. It was previously unheard of for a woman to stand up for herself and speak up for what she believed and wanted. When women are accused of being aggressive, what do we all tend to do? We shut up. We stop talking due to embarrassment or fear of developing a reputation of being aggressive. No one wants to be thought of that way, do we? So, I believe that most of the time, when people accuse women of being aggressive, it is done in a way to shut us up, and it works.

It has worked on me on a few occasions, and then I noticed that for fear of someone accusing me of being aggressive, I wouldn't speak up at all.. Holy cow, was that a slap in the face to wake me up when I realised what I was doing! This is when I started to do more research and reflect on my behaviour to decide if some of it was warranted and if I needed to learn to communicate better or find other ways to get my point across without interruption, being talked over or being accused of getting emotional and aggressive. I think, in all my career, I have only actually been called aggressive once, and when that happened, I think they had a point with 10% of what they were saying and 90% came down to the fact that I had been confident enough to speak up whilst they were worrying about how they didn't yet have a solution to the problem we were facing. When someone deflects a problem back to you, make sure you pause, stop, shut up and reflect on what you have said and why you think they would say what they said about you. Are you being aggressive, or do they just want to shut you up? Be honest with yourself and really challenge yourself about whether what they said is true. Then recompose yourself, gather your words in a positive factual way and re-present your brief.

We must remember that it wasn't too long ago that the norm for women was to be at home and looking after the family, and, because men earned the money to look after the family and home, men made all the decisions. If you don't believe me, consider that:

- It wasn't that long ago that orchestras were all-male, as the orchestral society didn't believe female musicians were good enough.

- According to the Royal Philharmonic Society, in 2022, only two British orchestras have a female principal conductor. Only six women conductors have titled roles amid the several hundred conductors on the staff of professional British orchestras. At last count, only 22 of the 371 conductors represented by British agents were female. That's 5.5%!

- Citigroup Inc. announced that Jane Fraser will succeed Mike Corbat as its CEO. Headlines hailed how Citibank had made history as the first big Wall Street bank to be run by a female—in 2020!

- The Royal Bank of Scotland announced that Alison Rose would become its first female CEO and the first to head up one of Britain's big four banks (RBS, HSBC, Barclays and Lloyds)—also in 2020!

- In Britain, women have been employed by banks since 1894, yet, over a century later, just around 30% of senior managers are female, according to the Bank of England.

If it took this long for women to get into senior leadership positions, no wonder it seems unusual for women to speak up in the workplace and be confident and assertive, and no wonder the rest of the world gives us the label "aggressive." They are not used to seeing women behaving this way, even when they believe it's OK for men. Phew, rant over! So, what do we do?

We become stronger, we become more confident, and as we do, we must be absolutely certain that we are communicating effectively.

I admit I have become very frustrated at times when people have cut across me and interrupted me when I was talking. Actually, not just frustrated—damn angry and pissed off because it's rude. It is basic respect and manners, and it has felt at times as if the only way I can stop it is to interrupt back.

However, I don't enjoy that. Interrupting back makes me feel aggressive and rude. It doesn't make me feel fulfilled at work, and I certainly don't want to feel like that or come across that way. When I reflect back on every single occasion when this has happened, I can criticise my own behaviour, too. Did I involve everyone in my thoughts and ideas before I gave the summary? Did I think about how requests affected how they felt? Did I allow the situation to press my buttons? Most importantly, what could I have done differently? Now, you might ask, why is it up to the women to change? An excellent question, and it isn't up to us to change, but how we behave, challenge and react to these situations *is* up to us.

A lot of industries are traditional, such as finance, law, certain manufacturing sectors, the military and other government sectors. Only in the last fifteen to twenty years or so have these industries even included women working in them, never mind encouraging them to pursue careers within them.

Society has to get used to the fact that women do want to be in the workplace and contribute just as much as men. We need new generations to accept these changes as normal.

Currently, it is against the norm for a woman to speak up and have the confidence to challenge situations in the workplace. It is against the norm to have a female CEO, and it is highly unusual for a woman to make it to the top and stay there. So, we have to be prepared to accept the challenge, as with challenge comes change.

However, things are indeed far better than they used to be, and we are definitely seeing more women in male-dominated industries. Here in the UK, we have had our own female prime minister, and let's not forget the most important thing: we have had a female reigning this country for seventy years (as of 2022)! Now, that is something we should all be proud of, whether you are a Royalist or not.

We must keep challenging these old traditions to make sure things keep moving forward, and we must support each other.

I believe that when a woman is being assertive and standing up for herself and expressing her beliefs, the main reason she gets accused of being aggressive is that the other person (usually a man) feels threatened by her from a talent point of view, not from a physical point of view. There's the fear that she might take his job, that she might know more than him, and therefore, the games begin.

I think it's very important, when you do have strong and confident views, that you also ensure that you are considerate of the other person's point and that you actively listen to the other person and are respectful; otherwise, if you are coming across as too strong, subconsciously talking and behaving as if everyone must agree with you or showing a disregard for others' opinions, then you are being slightly aggressive. Sometimes this can be hard, especially when others cut you off and talk over you to stop you from speaking; the danger here is that you respond by speaking more loudly to be heard and then getting angry or frustrated. This is when you can appear more aggressive, if you're not aware of it.

> *The key is to keep reminding yourself to be in control of your emotions, listen, speak clearly and re-confirm your viewpoint*

More and more, though, I am hearing stories of women being accused of being aggressive and, when they tell me the details, I find that they actually are! So, be honest, reflect on your own actions and ask yourself, *what could I have done better?*

What if you need to become more assertive?

There is a super book called *Alpha Assertiveness Guide for Men and Women* by Gerard Shaw, in which the author clearly defines the difference between assertive and aggressive. In the book, the author states that to be assertive, you must have personal empowerment and self-respect.

Believe in yourself and have clear goals and values, understand your own boundaries and set clear expectations. Assertiveness is a learned skill and, like any skill, it must be practised. An assertive style of communication includes how you think and speak, how you hold and conduct yourself, and the words you use. Being assertive includes your body language, so bear that in mind. How you stand, your facial expressions and your attitude (being relaxed but professional) all show that you are listening intently and engaging in conversation.

If you feel that you need to know more about learning to be more assertive, I strongly recommend you read Gerard Shaw's book. I always use the author's summary to remind myself of how to be assertive:

1) Know what you want, 2) say what you want and why, 3) to get what you want.

Always start with a positive feeling towards the problem. This is so crucial. Again, I've seen a massive difference in reaction if I start off negatively and defensively about a problem compared to starting it off positively, focusing on offering up solutions. Explain your thoughts and state the reasons why you think the way you do, and then end with your request for a new action or behaviour. Always finish with a positive ending, stating the benefits of your request.

But hold up . . . isn't that one of the problems, speaking up? Sometimes we daren't speak up and say what we want to say, as sometimes we know exactly what we want to say but we fear the outcome if we do say something. I can remember a few times when I didn't speak up, as the stress and fear around the reactions of those I was speaking with just wasn't worth it, or so I told myself. The fear rushing through my body, being embarrassed and then tongue-tied . . . ah, forget it! But, if I don't push through, what's the alternative?

> *1) Know what you want,*
> *2) Say what you want and why,*
> *3) To get what you want.*

Communication is everything, and you have to choose to be assertive, as this empowers you in every area of your life. This will help you to feel more confident, have more self-esteem and make better decisions for yourself and your family. Make sure you understand your own boundaries and values, as this is a very easy way to help you to become more confident and assertive without coming across as aggressive. At the same time, be careful not to be too assertive and over-confident. This can also be perceived as being more aggressive than assertive. Women get accused of this more than men do. We can become more emotional about a situation and, when this emotion becomes frustrating and we lose control of what we are trying to say or do, it can appear aggressive. This does apply to both men and women. Once we understand this and start to practise this behaviour, it is fascinating to see how others will change and react towards us.

From the research I have done for this book and from my own experience, I feel that there truly is an unconscious bias when talking about this in the workplace. I was staggered by the number of women who said that, during their performance reviews at work, they had received feedback about "appearing too aggressive" or needing to "just tone it down a bit—you're coming across aggressive."

I can usually sense that these comments are aimed at women similar to myself, who are more direct and logical in their conversation. Women are supposed to be more empathetic than men, but that doesn't mean you can't speak up, and that also doesn't mean people should give you a label just because you do!

This is where we need to create awareness and challenge the subject once it appears. I also find that everyone wants to be right when they're in the middle of a debate, and if a conversation is about trying to correct something that is wrong, the other party will naturally get defensive, so you need to be aware of this so that you don't respond abruptly but in a concise, factual and confident manner.

My old boss used to say, "Never, ever lose control and get angry; disappointed, yes, frustrated, maybe a little, but never angry. Anger leads to being aggressive, and being aggressive shows you're out of control. Who wants to communicate with someone who's out of control?"

CASE STUDY: Under-Performing Customer Service Levels

In a supply-chain meeting, the sales manager needed to address the service levels to a customer, as recently, levels had constantly been under 95%, which resulted in the supplier paying a fine on more than one occasion.

Sales Manager: "I really need to address our delivery performance, as this is the third time we have had to pay a fine, and it's becoming embarrassing. We could lose the business; this is the fault of the supply chain, and you really need to address it immediately."

While the circumstances around the failure in delivery performance is the responsibility of the supply chain, the last comment is not supportive of the whole team. The sales manager knows their desired outcome is to improve the customer service to this customer, but they don't know why there's an issue yet. Is it due to staff levels, factory breakdowns or customers not sticking to lead times when placing orders? Are orders above forecasts? When you know reasons, you can offer up solutions.

The end of the statement should have tried to show an understanding and concern about how a solution could be reached; how can the sales manager help by communicating with the customers? 99% of the time, the solutions are around communication. Maybe there was a vehicle breakdown and the team didn't inform the customer of the delay, or maybe they were out-performing forecasts but the team didn't ask the customer to review their sales and reflect the changes in the forecast. Maybe lead times were too short, in which case the sales manager needed to discuss this with the customer, addressing why they couldn't meet the lead times and how they could help. It's all communication.

A better ending would have been, "I really need to address our delivery performance, as this is the third time we have had to pay a fine, and it's costing the business money. What's causing the issues and how can I help to resolve it quickly?" Straight away, the sales manager would be offering help and offering to support the department involved. It's a positive ending to a negative situation.

Top Tips to Remember

1. Check in with yourself.

2. Prepare for the outcome you are looking for. What is it you want to achieve in your situation? What challenges could you face? What questions can you ask about the challenges? What solutions can you offer?

3. Practise what you want to say. What is your tone like? Are you talking too quickly or too slowly?

4. Ask for feedback to ensure you get people involved.

5. Be prepared to offer positive solutions, not negative obstacles.

6. Keep a check on how you feel. When assertiveness becomes aggressiveness, it's usually when we are challenged. When that happens, you may feel your heart race, you may talk too quickly to defend yourself, your hands may become clammy. If that happens in the moment, breathe slowly and ask yourself, *how can I express myself in a calm but assertive way?* Always watch out when this happens so you can learn and understand more of your own trigger points.

7. Know your outcome, including what you specifically want and why.

8. Deliver the solution and always thank people for listening to you and let them know that you appreciate their cooperation.

9. Prepare it, plan it and present it, and, of course, rehearse it.

10. Politeness always goes a long way.

Time to Reflect

Whether you need to be more assertive or less assertive, use this space to reflect on times when you wish you felt confident and assertive and how you would have behaved differently.

_____

_____

_____

_____

_____

_____

_____

_____

_____

_____

Go on, be brave and challenge yourself . . . start writing!

CHAPTER 6

How to Speak Up and Be Heard

Not being able to engage in meetings or feel empowered to speak up is one of the most common complaints in the workforce, and it comes from women more often than it does from men. Speaking up and sharing your ideas is one of the most empowering things you can do, and it is also one of the scariest things to do if you don't feel comfortable doing it. I titled this book *Why Won't You Let Me Speak?* not just to direct this question to the person or group on the other side of this conversation, but, more importantly, to direct it to *you!* **Why won't *you* let *you* speak?** Even when we have found the courage in our minds to speak up, sometimes we hold ourselves back for various reasons.

One of those reasons, and what's most frustrating, is when you eventually do speak up and someone has the nerve to interrupt you during your presentations, mid-flow in conversation, and shut you down. How damn rude!

There can be several reasons as to why this happens, and the majority of cases have shown that interrupting is done by men rather than women; not always, but that's usually the case. It relates to a power struggle, and when someone speaks over you by controlling the conversation, that person can feel like they have the power. You may have challenged their values or beliefs, or they may feel that they need to solve problems, yet they just don't know how to.

They may feel that they have the power to challenge you, believing that they have a different opinion that's better, or they may feel they have the power to close you down if they feel threatened by you. They may also feel they have the power to show that they know more than you. When this happens, it can make you feel unheard and not important enough to be listened to. It can make you feel insecure, not good enough at your job and not worthy of speaking up. It can make you feel anxious and make you start to doubt yourself, and this, in turn, knocks your self-confidence, so you stop talking.

This has happened to me often in one of two ways: 1) Wanting to speak up and comment on a subject, but then this wave of fear creeps over me and I don't say a word and then proceed to feel frustrated with myself for doing so for days after, or 2) I'm already talking in a meeting or during a presentation but someone interrupts me. I can't decide which is worse! Both of them have made me feel frustrated, annoyed and upset with myself and the person interrupting me, and I begin feeling reluctant to even try the next time without the feeling of nervousness and dread. In the end, I hit the "F**k it" button and shut up.

So first of all, how do you find the courage to speak up?

When the feeling of dread creeps over us, we usually feel waves of fear; fear of saying the wrong thing, fear that people will judge and fear of being wrong. Our palms start to sweat, our necks and faces become red, we worry that we might stutter, and our hands start to shake. The obvious thing to do is hit that f**k it button as the feeling of dread can be so overwhelming that we give up. So why do we do this when our desire is to speak up? What's really stopping us from just ignoring all of that and pushing through? I honestly do believe anyone can have the courage to speak up; we just need to learn how.

Confidence is usually the answer, and to feel more confident, we need to look at our self-esteem. Confidence is what we project to others, and our self-esteem is our own thoughts and feelings of self-worth and personal value. Confidence is a feeling of self-assurance about our ability and quality. Self-confidence is how we project ourselves, and self-esteem is how we feel about ourselves. You can be self-confident with low self-esteem, but to have courage, we need both a high level of self-esteem and a high level of self-confidence for it to feel congruent with ourselves and our values and for it to last.

> *Confidence is what we project to others and self-esteem is our own thoughts and feelings of self-worth and personal value.*

So how do we improve our self-esteem?

Our self-esteem is how we view ourselves; it's how we think and feel about ourselves. It can start from our childhoods, what we have learnt and what we have experienced. It can also be what we read and what others tell us. All of it begins with our thoughts, though. What do we think about ourselves? Do we believe our thoughts or are our thoughts and beliefs really someone else's, our mother's or our father's? Really challenge yourself to get to the truth. The only way to get your own self-esteem to a higher level is to work on it yourself. What thoughts are you thinking every day? There is so much research that suggests we have many thoughts a day—perhaps even between 15,000 and 70,000. That's a whole lot of thinking, so they'd better be damn good thoughts! But what if they aren't? What if 80% of our thoughts were negative? Now you can see why your self-esteem may be low! So, it's critical to try and understand what thoughts we are having that are making our self-esteem feel low. What conversations are we having in our heads?

You need to understand why you are thinking those thoughts in order to change them. Did you know we are the only species on the planet that has abstract thinking? I do always wonder how the heck researchers found that out! Seriously, how do they know if a cat or dog judges itself or has thoughts? Anyway, I digress, and I'd better move on before we really go deep into that subject!

Our brains are designed to predict the future and protect the present. In order to do this, they ask a lot of questions, especially to protect us. There are a lot of "What if?" questions. "What if" questions can create a lot of doubt if you are uncertain about something. *What if I don't say the right thing? What if they don't like me? What if they think my idea is rubbish?* Then, hey presto, you decide not to speak up at all. That's how it tends to work.

> *The good news is that if we can identify those thoughts and questions that don't serve us, then we can also change them to thoughts that do serve us.*

The thoughts we think and the words we speak can truly change our lives, for better or for worse. Only you can choose which direction to go in.

There are some great self-help books and videos that you can quickly learn from to help you in this area. YouTube has many, so check them out to help you learn how to improve your own self-esteem, and remember: these are your thoughts and your questions and you control them, so choose wisely and change them quickly! As soon as your self-esteem grows, so will your self-confidence.

What to Do with an Interrupter

So how do you deal with an interrupter? You'll start to notice in this book that a pattern emerges where all of these steps are interlinked with one another. Being interrupted has happened to me so many times that sadly I started to interrupt back; this is a big mistake! Do not do this. It only made the situation worse, every single time.

I would interrupt back; I would feel angry that the person had interrupted and that they had taken over my conversation and then I would try to be assertive but come across as aggressive. And then I would be accused of getting too emotional! Each of these steps can lead on to the next and the next until *you* take control of them. Taking control in a constructive, positive way does take more practice and patience, but it's worth it in the long run.

It is imperative not to interrupt someone but rather control how you respond. Control your emotions, your frustrations and your reactions, as the only person you are ever in control of is you.

So, what do you do?

The situation depends on the environment you are in, whether it's a conversation in a meeting or giving a presentation. Either way, remember your own manners; don't interrupt the interrupter. Remember to treat others how you would want to be treated.

Wait for the pause, listen first, and then speak, or, if that fails, deliberately pause again, raise your hand if you need to (as this makes a deliberate point), and then "ask" to speak.

Pause and then speak clearly about what you want to say.

As tempting as it is, when you experience being shut down or spoken over, learn how to use the pauses to then speak but never interrupt. Remember your manners and, at all times, remember to treat people how you would want to be treated. If you don't want to be interrupted, don't interrupt others. This can be tough for some people, as it was for me! I have strong opinions, but I soon realised that I get further faster by taking these steps—plus, when I did, I enjoyed my job more!

> *Pause and then speak clearly about what you want to say;*
> *a) know what you want,*
> *b) say what you want,*
> *c) get what you want.*

By pausing and counting to ten before you react, you allow your brain to check in with what's going on. Slow breathing calms your heart rate down and gives you just enough time to quickly assess the situation. Sometimes we all react too quickly, which can make a situation worse. If we stop and check in with what's going on, we can prevent that. Think, think and think again as to what's occurring and make sure you understand or seek further clarity, as this can allow you to react in perhaps a different way and also bide more time to think through how you want to react.

> *Pause, stop and think.*

I learnt a great technique called "The Work" from an author called Byron Katie. She uses four questions to try to really understand what it is we are thinking, as sometimes we can overthink, analyse too much and come up with our own scenarios in situations that might be far from the actual truth.

1. Is it true?
2. Can you absolutely know that it's true?
3. How do you react when you believe that thought?
4. Who would you be without the thought?

To be fair, I usually get to question two and wonder if I should have been in theatre and the performing arts, given the way some things come across at times! I usually defend my answer to question two beyond a shadow of a doubt, as I seriously do think it's right. I'm passionate and driven, so of course it's right! But seriously, asking yourself these questions is a great tool when you feel your mouth getting ready to go into fourth gear! Now that I ask myself these questions, I usually get to question two and it stops me dead in my tracks. It allows me time to reflect, and it usually changes my approach. It takes the emotion out of the situation and allows me to think more clearly.

Other Peoples Perspectives

I saw this image on Facebook once, and it really drives home how two people can be looking at the same thing, but both conclude completely different things and be absolutely adamant about it.

"Seek first to understand, then to be understood," - the quote by Stephen R. Covey is a phrase I repeat to myself often. It's from his book, *The 7 Habits of Highly Effective People,* another great classic, which I reread every year or so.

I recently had a situation where I simply could not get the other person to see the common sense in a situation where a suggestion was indeed going to make their life far easier in a change of process that we were both using. It was driving me mad.

I checked in with other colleagues and associates, who reaffirmed my ideas as the right course of action. They were common sense; they were relevant and they would be so simple to implement and use. Could I get the other person to agree? No, not at all. This went on for weeks, and I just could not see what was going wrong. I kept thinking of changing my approach, my style, using other people to help, but none of it worked. I concluded the other person was just downright stubborn and, no matter what I did, he would never change.

Until one day, my partner hit me in the face with a wet fish! Well, not exactly, but it sure felt like it.

During COVID-19, I had been working from home for a year, like most people. Well, I was hanging around with myself, and I spotted that my language became about *me*. "I want this to happen," "I think you should," "I think it's reasonable," "I know it will be better..." What happened? I stopped talking about *us*, the team, using "we," and asking for feedback.

As soon as I changed my language, magic happened. I started to ask for feedback from the whole team so "we" could be more productive. I asked the person I had been speaking with, "What do you think *we* should do?" The difference was amazing. He responded with what he wanted, and guess what? It was exactly the same thing I did!

The whole process was exhausting, but what a simple mistake to rectify! So, make sure you also refer back to what's in it for the other person and how your proposal will benefit everybody. Always talk as a team and always deliver solutions for others and not just for yourself.

Two Ears and One Mouth

Communicate in balance with what you were born with: two ears and one mouth! Today everybody wants to talk, including me. However, we will learn a heck of a lot more if we listen. By listening to the other person, you are sending so many messages to them.

You're being respectful and polite; you're showing that you care, that you're interested. You value what they have to say, which makes them feel valued too. When they feel valued, it opens them up to respond to you in the same way, so both parties are open to discussions.

Sometimes, we only listen to respond, and we are all very guilty of that. We are preparing what we want to say and how we will say it. Sometimes, this is because we are defensive about what we are hearing, and sometimes it's because we're excited to share a similar experience.

When dealing with any situation and, in particular, difficult conversations, it helps to "first seek to understand and then to be understood." Once you understand the other person's thoughts, you can present yourself in a way that is in alignment with how they are thinking.

> *Listen to understand; don't listen to respond.*

Your Body Language Speaks More Than Your Words!

If you want to be heard, remember to include your body language. Remember, if 7% of all communication is verbal, 37% is your voice, then 55% comes from your body language! That's a high percentage of how we communicate, so we had better understand what we are "saying" with our body language to ensure we do not give the wrong impression.

Can I confess something, just between me and you? I am very, very expressive with my face. My muscles move up and down, left and right, with every word I speak. The problem with that is that I can't lie because my face will surely tell you that I am lying! My face also tells you if I'm sad but trying to talk positively, and it tells you when I'm mad but trying to be calm.

If I'm thinking but my thoughts are, shall we say, not quite positive about the person in front of me, my face will always tell you the truth. I remember being in a meeting where someone else was talking and I didn't quite understand what they meant in their debate. As I was thinking and wondering about their words and meanings, I was puzzled and confused. Unbeknownst to me, that expression was on my face, *all over my face*, flashing in neon lights. My arms were folded, and the person speaking asked me, "You're looking angry. What didn't you like about that?"

I was mortified! I wasn't feeling "angry," I just didn't understand the subject, and I certainly wasn't going to ask about it until I did a bit of research after the meeting. I blushed with embarrassment, opened my mouth to speak and stuttered, "Oh, oh, nothing, it's just, oh, the sun is shining through the blinds and I can't see properly to hear you!" What? *I can't see properly to hear you?* Well, that was a good line to give. Anyway, my point here is to make sure you are aware of your own body language; otherwise, you might be sending out the wrong message, just like my colleague Jessica did with a client at a lunch meeting once. Unknown to us, Jessica's boyfriend was also at the restaurant with his friends and, by coincidence, had a table right opposite us. As lunch was served, Jessica's boyfriend kept winking at her and, likewise, she winked back, playing with her hair, twisting it around her fingers and flirting with him . . . except there was one major problem. Our client thought she was doing it to him!

Body language can give off the totally wrong message. It can also make you feel confident or insecure, strong or weak. Our own physiology not only communicates how we feel to others, but certain changes in our physiology can also affect the way we actually feel. Think of a moment where you were so sad your heart nearly burst. Remember how you stood. Where was your head? How did you feel? I bet your shoulders were slumped, your head was hanging low and your arms were maybe hanging by your side or resting on your legs, or you were giving yourself a cuddle by folding your arms. Thinking of that, you feel low and sad, right? Now, remember a moment when you felt proud of yourself; passing your driving test or exams, getting that promotion. What was your physiology like then? Standing tall, shoulders back and relaxed, maybe your hands on your hips, back straight, head held high, and *wow*, what a different feeling! I bet you felt strong and confident and like you could take on the world! *The world*, I hear you cry! Tony Robbins talks about your power move and getting yourself in the right state of mind and energy at the start of each day or before a meeting. By putting yourself in the right state, it changes your energy and shifts your focus. When you do this, the whole outcome for your day starts in a positive frame of mind, positive energy rather than negative energy, meaning your day is highly likely to be a good one, achieving everything that you have set out to do.

Amy Cuddy, in her TED talk, "Your body language may shape who you are," really explains how a power pose can change your mindset and energy and make you feel more confident, more assertive and more positive. Watch the talk; it's about twenty minutes long, but will transform how you feel if you try what she suggests.

Think about when you see a marathon runner crossing the finish line, or a footballer scoring a goal, and remember how their bodies are posed: their arms are up in the air in a V-shape. Maybe that's V for Victory, but when we feel a sense of achievement, our bodies are more alert and alive and we feel fantastic. If we feel more alert, we will give off this positive energy, speak with a more positive and enthusiastic approach, and, guess what—people will want to listen and interact with us. So, try out the Wonder Woman power pose that Amy Cuddy talks about.

Next time you're getting ready to go into a meeting or to have that conversation with your partner or your children or your in-laws . . . check your body language. Stand tall, put your hands on your hips, smile and put on your invisible Wonder Woman outfit because you've got this; now go and get it!

I remember the first time I stood up to answer a question at a conference. There were around 200 people there, with ten people on a roundtable. We had been working in groups on presentation skills. That was the easy part for me; I could write down all the features and benefits of the product and create that presentation that kept people engaged, and I could easily present in front of two to five people without feeling nervous. Sounds great, doesn't it? But, with any more people than five, *here it goes again!* That's what I used to say to myself.

My heart started racing, I began to sweat. Actually, at this point, you really need to know that I do not sweat, not normally. Not even in normal situations where you would expect it, like at the gym or on a run or a bike; no, not me. I just glisten!

So, when I knew it was my turn to speak, for some bizarre reason I would start to sweat. This made me even more self-conscious. But I thought, *NO!* Not this time. I had worked hard on this, and I wanted to be confident and stand up and present for our table. So, I did. But I didn't exactly stand up, writhing to my feet like Bambi trying to walk for the first time. As I lifted my hand, I knocked my notes off the table, and I stood up but couldn't see my notes.

My shoulders slumped, and I even bent my knees slightly to get close to the floor so I could see my notes . . . I must have looked bonkers! Because I was standing that way, my head was low, my voice was quiet and my words stuttered out.

Remember what I said about other people's body language and how you can read what they are thinking without them speaking? Well yes, just one look up and I could tell. Blank stares, raised eyebrows, squinting eyes like they felt they couldn't or didn't want to hear my words. One guy had his hands on his head! For crying out loud, it was just a mess.

I sat down and said to myself, *Never, ever again am I going to speak up!!* But then, as I sat there, it hit me. No wonder I couldn't speak up, standing like that! No wonder people couldn't hear me and lost interest. It was the way I held myself! I decided that next time, I would focus on my stance. I know my words and I know what to say and how to say it, so I would use my power pose.

Later in the week, we had another session, and I did exactly that. I stood up, I held my head up and I started off with my hands on my hips as I began to speak. I didn't keep them there, as it would have looked too fierce, but as I spoke, I knew it was going to go well. People looked on with intrigue as I continued, and I used hand gestures with my words and my presentation flowed brilliantly. After, a few people came up to me and said, "Wow, what happened to you?!" "You are so different compared to when you stood up on Monday," and, "You looked and sounded so much more confident!" I was beaming, and all just because of how I had stood and embraced my power pose.

> *Stand tall, put your hands on your hips, smile and put on your invisible Wonder Woman outfit. You've got this; now go and get it!*

Top Tips to Remember

1. Always, always check in with yourself to ensure you are being calm, confident and respectful; if you find it still doesn't work, you must keep practising.

2. Here are a few strategies if someone interrupts you whilst you're giving a presentation. Say to them . . .

   a) "Thanks for engaging, but I'll finish what I'm currently talking about and then we can discuss it." Being firm and confident in your voice will stop the interruption; if it doesn't and they try again, raise your palm (this indicates a "stop" sign) and just simply repeat yourself.

   b) "Please can you not interrupt me until I've finished? Then we can hear and explore your views." This approach is great, as it's very hard for the other person to say no.

   c) "Thanks for interrupting me; can I now continue?" And always smile. Everyone knows it's rude to interrupt, so hopefully, by just highlighting this fact, it will remind others not to interrupt. By pausing, you are allowing them to speak, so they should then allow you to carry on.

3. Remember not to interrupt others either; let them speak. Remember how it makes you feel when someone doesn't let you get a word in edgeways!

4. Is anyone really stopping you from speaking up, or do you need to realign what you want? Practise how you will say what it is you want. Get feedback from others, especially your colleagues or friends. Be respectful to others. Take your time.

5. Check in with your state. Are you excited or feeling negative? Check back in with what you want.

6. Get into your power pose; don't forget your posture.

7. Dress in your favourite confident clothes.

8. Be kind, be polite and smile.

9. Remember, there is always a way in any situation. You can find a way.

Time to Reflect

What does your body language look like? Look in the mirror and observe how you stand. In a meeting, be aware of how you sit. What can you do to improve your own body language? No, don't go and put on your diamond ball dress to work . . . OK, go for it, why not? You be you, girl!

CHAPTER 7

---◆◆◆---

#ChoosetoChallenge—Why Do I Have to Make the Tea?

Most men in today's work environment don't realise when there are issues with their own behaviour or comments, so don't shy away from asking or challenging why they are showing gender inequality, as half the time they probably don't even know it. This is called unconscious bias.

When the #MeToo campaign happened and the #BlackLivesMatter campaign started, so many people commented on how they didn't realise that some of their own behaviours and thoughts were not even their own and they didn't even know what they meant. They were comments or beliefs given to them by their parents, culture and society. What you read or hear in the media can also influence your values and beliefs. Even when they challenged the source of some of their beliefs, they still didn't realise that they were being sexist or racist and what damage their old learned behaviours could do. If we don't challenge some of these beliefs, we will never change the way people think and behave around racism and sexism and many other areas of discrimination. Even when we do, it will take years to create lasting change. Generations may need to change in order for new values and beliefs to filter through. In some cases, it isn't just men who can have unconscious bias; it can be women, too.

> *Unconscious bias is a learned attitude, assumption or belief that exists in our unconscious minds. It plays a huge role in decision-making and forming our opinions. Be aware of it, challenge it and realign it*

At first, it may feel uncomfortable to challenge people and company cultures when you hear negative statements or assumptions. When I come across moments like this, I always start with "I'm curious as to why you would say that. What makes you think that way?" Just one question can make someone stop and think. They will automatically search their brains for their reasoning, and they will either notice what they are saying is inappropriate and change it or they won't. If they don't, I just ask more questions, and usually, it ends with them addressing and changing the way they think.

Sometimes, when I have used the word "challenge" with people, they have said they find even the word "challenge" confrontational. They feel threatened even by the word alone and feel afraid to be challenged. If you approach the situation by asking questions, it can take a certain element of pressure off your own feelings towards the challenging moments. Become intrigued, as it is amazing how both parties can learn something new from each other.

These are the questions I use to challenge any situation:

1. Why would you want to take this approach?
2. How have you made this assumption in your own mind?
3. Why do you think that's appropriate?
4. How can we move forward without being biased in our approach?
5. Are you making this decision because I'm gender/race?

I usually only use this last question as a final resort to address an issue if the other questions don't work. Be careful when doing this, as the other person will not want to be accused of being sexist or racist and will start to become defensive. By the time you get to question 5, the other person has probably realised that they are coming across with a biased point of view. Around 80% of the time, it is an innocent mistake or lack of understanding as to how they are coming across to you, but you must challenge them and call them out on it. If you don't, how can we ever expect things to change? If the person gets too defensive, this is an opportunity to suggest discussing the problem with other members of the team, asking for another point of view and involving HR (if appropriate and only as a last resort).

On occasion, it might be worth considering using the term "we" and referring to the situation as a team unconscious bias issue so that the other person doesn't feel so challenged. For example:

1. Do you think we are being biased in our approach?
2. How can we ensure that we are being fair and not sexist or racist?
3. What grounds are we taking on this approach?
4. What are our other options?

Of course, it all depends on the situation at hand, but no matter what the situation, nine times out of ten, asking questions will highlight the area of concern and the other person may just acknowledge that their behaviour needs to change. Just asking the questions makes people stop and think. Questions are very powerful, as they do stop people's opinions from driving the conversation. They open them up to other possibilities. You cannot use gender-related questions every time you get an objection, though—only when it's appropriate. You don't want to be known for throwing the female card all the time. Other types of questions can be:

1. Why do you think it's appropriate for me to do this work instead of Mike?
2. What's the difference between John and me making the tea today?
3. Shall we take turns getting lunch?

4. How about we let Gary take the notes and I time keep us to the agenda?

Most importantly, discuss, debate and challenge any situation you are faced with that you want to change with a close member of your team, friends and family. Also, remember that you also need to be objective and neutral when explaining the situation. There are times and occasions when someone's thoughts and opinions aren't an unconscious bias reaction; we just need to sometimes face a situation and try another approach to communicate better around a problem area.

> *Just asking questions makes people stop and think. Questions are very powerful, as asking them does stop people's opinions from driving conversations. Asking questions opens them up to other possibilities.*

One of the main reasons why, as women, we find ourselves going along with doing things such as always making the tea, taking notes or not speaking up when we want is that there is a strong desire to please people. Our natural tendency is to please people because if we do, then we'll be liked; it's as simple as that. In fact, people-pleasing is a trait of men, too. So many of us worry that if we don't say yes and please the other party, we won't be liked. The most fundamental basic need of a human being is to feel loved, to be liked and feel needed. We need to be aware of what we are saying yes to and what we should say no to.

Women are largely humanity's caretakers, and we are taught to be more passive and less aggressive; plus, a people-pleasing woman will not likely be labelled high-maintenance or "difficult." She would rather bend over backwards than appear fussy.

A people-pleaser has an emotional need to please other people, even at the expense of their own needs and desires. People-pleasing is a way to feel connected, needed and wanted by other people, and it usually comes from a lack of confidence and self-esteem. People-pleasers can end up resentful, dissatisfied and depressed.

This can be changed by first being aware of when you are people-pleasing. Once you become aware, you can identify why you are doing it. You can then create new beliefs and habits around when you do it.

For example, when your manager asks you to do another piece of work but you are already busy trying to meet deadlines, your normal thought reaction may be to say yes to please your boss. Your thoughts may reaffirm this belief, as they may tell you, "Do this work so she knows you like her," "If you do this, she will like you," or "Do this and you will become an important member of her team." But what if you try and do the work and you miss the deadline? What if it affects your other work so that you miss those deadlines, too?

So, you work late in the evening and over the weekend and then wonder why you're tired and feel rundown. You can't sleep, and bad habits creep in. *I'll just have one more glass of wine to help me relax, maybe one more to help me sleep.* You wake up with a rough head, and then the day starts all over again.

I had a client who gets burned out every two to three years. She doesn't know how to say no. She always says yes to the workload and openly admits it's to please her boss. It doesn't please her boss or her work colleagues when she goes off sick for two months to recover from burnout. Nor does her body say thank you, as every year she gets run down with severe colds, flu and chest infections. As women, sometimes we want to prove ourselves as superheroes, and this is due to the pushback against women being good enough to climb the career ladder. Sometimes it isn't even just about having a career; it's about loving the job you're in and being afraid of losing it.

You can see the theme again here, which goes back to self-confidence and self-esteem. Feel the fear and don't be pushed into doing something you don't want to do because even if you do, you would feel like crap, so you are no better off.

The way to help with this situation is to ask questions. Here is a scenario that I have run into time and time again, and I hear this from colleagues, friends and clients all the time. This response works a treat.

"I can do this work for you. Which is more important: to hit the deadline for Report A or Report B?"

I have asked this question and gotten the answer "Both!" *Ahhhh! Seriously?*

If so, I still ask more questions. "OK, but which one is more important?"

The question allows the other person to take stock and really ask themselves which one is more important. Sometimes it can still go further, and you can be told both reports need to be done on time.

A brilliant question when you get this stubborn response is, "OK, that can be done, but the research into the report won't be as intense due to the time allowed for it, and I know you want me to do my best work, so which one do you want me to focus more on? What other help can you give me in order to meet both deadlines?"

> *Get creative and think differently. You can always find a way!*

Focus your mind on what you want to happen and the outcome you want to achieve to do the best job you can, and always remember the following:

1. Know what you want,
2. Say what you want to,

3. Get what you want. Have a direct talk with yourself and be clear and concise.

There are many examples of when you need to #choosetochallenge. Another example is being asked to always take notes in a meeting when there are also men who could take do this. If this happens, agree to do it on the first occasion and politely request that notetaking is done in turns each time you meet. Be aware, though, that the request might simply be because you can actually do the task at hand better than the men can! Sometimes you just need to suck it up and get on with it; life can be tough and we *can* deal with it.

On a more serious note, there are occasions when you must call out inappropriate behaviour: sexual harassment.

Sexual harassment is a form of unlawful discrimination under the Equality Act 2010. The law says something is sexual harassment if the behaviour is meant to or has the effect of violating your dignity or creating an intimidating, hostile, degrading, humiliating or offensive environment. However, the law has gone one step further to try and stop sexual harassment before it gets to this stage.

In March 2019, the Council of Europe Committee of Ministers adopted a Recommendation on Preventing and Combating Sexism. The text contains the first-ever internationally-agreed-upon definition of sexism. It also proposes a set of concrete measures to combat sexism through legislation and policies and awareness-raising. The definition of sexism provided is: "Any act, gesture, visual representation, spoken or written words, practice or behaviour based upon the idea that a person or a group of persons is inferior because of their sex, which occurs in the public or private sphere, whether online or offline, with the purpose or effect of: i. violating the inherent dignity or rights of a person or a group of persons; or ii. resulting in physical, sexual, psychological or socioeconomic harm or suffering to a person or a group of persons; or iii. creating an intimidating, hostile, degrading, humiliating or offensive environment; or iv. constituting a barrier to the autonomy and full realisation of human rights by a person or a group of persons; or v. maintaining and reinforcing gender stereotypes. This includes comments, jokes and behaviours that are also classed as 'Subtle Sexism.'"

The EU Council suggested that sexism at work involves:

- Derogatory comments
- Objectification
- Sexist humour or jokes
- Overfamiliar remarks
- Silencing or ignoring people
- Gratuitous comments about dress and physical appearance
- Sexist body language
- Lack of respect

Call it out and #Challenge.

This of course does not mean that, as women, we can dress however we want and not expect men to take notice. Showing far too much cleavage will get women staring at your breasts too, never mind men, so we need to play our part. Somebody once said to me that "I should be able to dress as I like, and it's the other person who has the problem!" Be that as it may, this debate over how a woman should or should not dress has been going on for hundreds of years and we just need to be a little bit more sensible and dress for appropriate occasions. If you want to show your cleavage at work, expect men and women to stare at your breasts. Where else can they look? If you wear a short skirt, people will look and stare at your legs. If you want to be listened to and for people to focus on what you are saying, don't give them another distraction. It's as simple as that.

There are occasions where we can also take things so literally that poor guys daren't ask us to do anything without worrying about being accused of being sexist, so don't sweat the small stuff either.

If someone asks you to print something off for him, is it a sexist comment because females are there to do menial tasks, or is he asking you because you are the only person around who can help him? The more you think about something, the more prominent it becomes. The more upset you get, guess what? The more upsetting it becomes. You become what you think about. Instead, think, *My mind, my thoughts . . . What's the most important thing to do right now?* Address the situation or move on?

I'm not saying ignore it. But don't overthink it. Overthinking something can make you anxious and stressed. It drains you of your energy and distracts you from the most important things. When you catch yourself overthinking, you need to take control of your thoughts and call yourself out in your own mind to stop those thoughts.

Visualise a stop sign and switch your thoughts to something more positive and calming. Focus on your breath, slow it down and give yourself a pep talk. Choose your own phrase that empowers you, such as, "Move on to the important things" or "Will this be so important to me in two weeks' time?" If the answer is yes, then start looking for the solution and don't dwell on the problem. Studies have shown—and I know from experience—that when we feel depressed or anxious, one of the best things for the mind is to start problem-solving.

When you even just think about problem-solving, the brain begins searching for answers, and it is incredible how creative you'll find yourself being with this simple technique. If you can, find time to take a ten-to-fifteen-minute break, get some fresh air and go for a walk. This in itself distracts the mind and allows you to stop overthinking.

When challenging a situation, you don't want to sound like you're just moaning and whining. You need to think through what you want to say and stop thinking about what you don't want and how you can empower not just yourself but the other person to take action and change. You want to get this person on board, to see reason and to encourage them or the business to change. You can't achieve this if you are just moaning at them.

> *You must start with a positive sentence, state the problem and end with a solution*

For example, "James, I think you're excellent at running meetings and holding people to their timeslots when talking and your enthusiasm keeps the meetings alive. I just wonder why every time we have a meeting you ask me to take the minutes when there are five men in the room. I know you're always fair about these sorts of things; can I suggest we all take it in turns?" This way James cannot offer up a reason as to why it should be you carrying out this task every time.

Top Tips to Remember

1. Be aware—are you a people-pleaser? Do you really have to make the tea or do you offer it through unconscious behaviour?
2. Can you actually say no as well as saying yes?
3. Just because you once believed something you were told doesn't mean it is true.
4. Be confident and self-assured.
5. Engage and say what you want and why.
6. Be brave and say what you want to happen next.
7. Find a support group.
8. Plan how you will change.
9. Rehearse what you want to say.
10. Find a mentor group.

Time to Reflect

What situations do you feel you need to challenge at work? What questions can you ask?

_____

_____

_____

_____

_____

_____

_____

_____

_____

_____

_____

_____

Be brave, be confident. You can do this; we've got your back!

CHAPTER 8

・❖・

You Become Who You Hang Around With—Watch Out!

If you want to improve your network of friends and acquaintances, then go and hang out where they do. For example, if you want to be a better speaker, attend the Toastmasters weekly get-together in your area. If you want to learn about entrepreneurship, then join a local breakfast club and go and meet people who can advise and help you. Likewise, if you find that you're hanging out too much at the coffee shop and spending too much time just gossiping and it's getting you down, then stop going.

I was convinced that I needed to fit in and, if I wanted to climb the career ladder, then I had to be like those around me. When I look back, it really was a crazy thing to do, and I fell into this trap on several different occasions. As the old saying goes, "You become who you hang around with," but my problem was that I've always worked in male-dominated industries, from the motor industry to manufacturing, and yes, I did find myself changing—and not for the better. I became more masculine in how I dressed and how I spoke. I remember thinking that if I behaved like the men, they'd start to accept me. I ditched the blouse for a jumper, the skirt for trousers and the heels for boots. I did this as I didn't want to be accused of dressing in a flirtatious way to get to the top. You know the style: short skirts, too much cleavage. I wanted people to listen to what I had to say, not stare at my chest every time I spoke!

I started to lose my feminine edge. I became more bottled up and lost my authentic self. I even found myself watching the football results on a weekend so I could join in with the conversation in the office. I hated football! I started to swear in conversation like the men did, until one day, someone asked me, "Why do you swear so much?" I was twenty at the time, and I was devastated, as I didn't even realise I was doing it! I have no idea why I would belittle myself like that, and I guess it was because I thought it would make me sound like the men and, if I did, they would accept me, and if I was accepted, then my career would grow. Eventually, it did, but I soon became accused of being aggressive. It's still odd to think that a man can swear and not be called aggressive, but when a woman does, she is called aggressive. My nana once said that when someone swears, it's because they are not intelligent enough to express themselves properly! I thought, *crikey, now they don't think I'm intelligent!* I then stopped swearing for a while, although I guess we all have our moments when we still do!

It did become confusing, figuring out how I was supposed to behave at times. I thought if I wanted to learn more, I needed to hang around with people who had achieved career progression, and maybe that wasn't those I worked with; maybe I could learn more from outside work. I started to read more books and watch more TED talks.

If you don't know about TED talks, TED is a non-profit organisation whose mission is to make great ideas accessible in videos that last around eighteen minutes or less. They have a whole catalogue of free videos from the world's most inspiring leaders on many different topics. Speakers include scientists, philosophers, musicians, business and religious leaders, philanthropists and many others. You can learn things so quickly from TED talks that I highly recommend them for many areas in work and life.

As you can gather by now, I am quite impatient, and these talks are brilliant for me, as they give me a quick, brief summary from a speaker. Then, if I like them and the subject intrigues me, I research the speaker a bit more. I usually end up buying a book or a course, but, most importantly, the talks have given me a great connection to people who are interested in and passionate about the same things I am.

I began to connect with more people who were interested in the same subjects I was and then, as if by magic, everything started to make sense and click into place.

Yes, you most definitely become who you hang around with, so choose carefully!

> *Only embrace further connection with people if their values and beliefs align with your own*

I started to understand what I was doing and decided that it's important to be yourself. This begins with your own self-confidence, and this must start with knowing what you want and why you want it and practising your communications skills so, no matter what circumstances you find yourself in at work or in your personal life, you have the skills to communicate what you want.

As Jim Rohn once said, "You are the average of the five people you spend the most time with." Hang around with those people that hold you to a higher standard. Find networking groups and breakfast clubs. There are also some really great groups on LinkedIn and Facebook.

Beware of even your close family and friends. Sometimes they don't want to see you succeed and are quite jealous of you having the strength of character to want to succeed in areas of your life. God bless her, I remember my mum saying, "Why on earth do you want that promotion and want to work so hard? You should be at home cooking dinner!" My own mother! But people have different desires in life, and just because yours are different from theirs, that does not mean that yours are wrong. Don't let that influence or stop you. Find some women's support groups that can help you.

> *The more women can support each other, the stronger we will feel, the more confident we will become and the happier we will be, not just in the workplace but outside of it, too*

Find a group that suits you, as there will be one. I did go to quite a few and wondered what the heck I was doing at some. There was one group where the leader asked all the women to stand in a circle and sing a welcome song. Sorry, but no . . . that is not for me and it's not what I went for! Other groups were like having afternoon tea with my Aunt Mary, talking about everything except the very subjects we wanted to, and another talked negatively about everything that was wrong with no focus on what we could do to improve things. But do not give up! Find a group that thinks like you, has guest speakers on subjects you want to hear about and embraces your thoughts and input. LinkedIn has many good groups, so do your research.

I am a strong believer that you do become who you hang around with, so invest your time wisely. Join support groups and industry associations and get in touch with me and I'll help you find one. Our details are at the end of the book.

But you must do the work; there is no one coming to rescue you. Put in the work, take action, learn the skills and there will be no stopping you!

Top Tips to Remember

1. Learn to be proud of who you are.
2. If your friends do not support you, find new ones.
3. Find working groups and network in your industry.
4. Find a coach or a mentor.
5. Take more self-development courses and read more books.
6. Remind yourself of all that you want to be, do and have.
7. Watch TED talks that interest you.
8. Keep a goal journal and keep checking in.
9. Know what you want.
10. Grab life with both hands—you are amazing. Go live your dreams.

Time to Reflect

Who is your biggest influence in life? Do you need to upscale some of your friends if they're bringing you down? Who else can you talk to and connect to? What groups can you research and join?

_____

_____

_____

_____

_____

_____

_____

_____

_____

_____

_____

CHAPTER 9

————— ❖ —————

Understand Your Audience and Connect to Them

Whilst this is a short chapter, it is a very important one if you are doing presentations at work and you are involved in meetings and are part of a team. There are a number of ways of presenting your information depending on the type of audience you are talking to.

For example, if you want to launch a new way of doing things at work and the process involves different teams from sales, customer service, operations and finance, make sure you talk to each team that is affected and, when you do, make sure that you talk about the benefits in their relevant area of work. Ask them if they see any issues or have ideas on how to do it better.

You have to connect with your audience and learn to understand what they want from you as much as what you want from them. Why should they help you? What's in it for them? You will always get support when you show people what's in it for them as well as the company. Again, it's about communication, connection and relationships.

If you can communicate in a way that connects with the individual or team, you can build a relationship together, which makes it far easier to get things done. Think about their roles and goals and how what you are doing helps them to achieve their goals. If you are talking to an engineering team, be very factual and orderly; you will lose their attention and focus if you start talking about consumer trends and the sales benefits of the new product! And if you're talking to an operations team about a new product you're thinking about developing, don't talk for too long about the marketing or you'll lose them. Make your conversation relevant to their area of work and you'll engage them.

You may be talking to an audience of experts in your field. Plan how you want to communicate with them. What do you want to achieve? What result do you want or what action do you want them to take? What does your audience already know about the subject?

What will your audience value and what will their attitude be? Be prepared for any questions you may get. Also, watch their body language and facial expressions, as these things alone give you feedback to react to. If someone is looking puzzled as you are talking, stop and ask them why. This shows you care and value their input and it also gives you a chance to re-clarify and even reposition the points you are making.

Do your research about your audience. You can research them online or ask around about them. You may find out they have just got married or been on a holiday, which means you can ask them questions about those things to help build your rapport.

If you're talking to an audience, ask who the audience is and what they are expecting to hear. I was once asked to do a talk on the functionality of food in manufacturing and how it impacts an industry, only to find out that the audience was full of people who were farmers and industry press. They didn't really care what was going on in the industry further down the supply chain; they wanted to know how they could improve their own businesses. I think if I had talked about protein structures and whipability and emulsification properties, the farmer who looked after his organic hens would have fallen asleep in ten minutes. So just be sure you are talking about the right subject to the right audience.

The most important part of any type of communication is that it is the process of delivering messages between people. It's all about people. I know that, with some people, if I give a detailed account of how I got to my summary, they are just not interested; they just want to be told what to do. On the other hand, I know some people don't want to hear just the summary; they want me to justify and prove my summary.

Get to know your audience and adapt your communication so you can connect with them; the difference will be amazing.

Always thank your audience for their time. Everyone is so busy and for you to acknowledge and show your gratitude that they took time out of their own busy schedule to come and listen to you will make sure that they know you value them and their time.

Top Tips to Remember

1. Research your audience.
2. Work out their communication style preference.
3. Connection is the most important aspect of communication.
4. Ask open questions if you can't research people beforehand.
5. Get to know your audience to be able to then understand them.
6. Involve them.
7. Be aware of their body language.
8. Challenge and ask for feedback.
9. Adapt where necessary.
10. Always thank the audience for their time and attention.

Time to Reflect

Who is your audience? Is it a team member, your children or your partner? How do they communicate? Can you pick up a style? What do they want to know and what do you want to say? How can you improve? What's the next step you will take to know your audience better?

_____

_____

_____

_____

_____

_____

_____

_____

_____

_____

_____

CHAPTER 10

Find Your Authentic Voice and Say Goodbye to the Imposter!

This has to be my favourite chapter because I really connect with it, as I have experienced it at some level nearly every single day!

Imposter syndrome is the belief that, to others, you are not as competent as you actually are. Imposter syndrome is based on fear of failure or fear of being caught out that you're not who you think you are. It can make you feel unworthy, and this can lead to feelings of anxiety and depression. That's all it is—a belief that you have. Actually, it's also a belief that society wants us to have. In my experience, men also have this but for some reason, they don't get the label as much as women, so be careful how we label ourselves when, in fact, all we are dealing with is fear.

The imposter is our minds, our own thoughts. It's our inner thoughts and fears being brought to life in our minds. It is a protection zone that *thinks* it needs to shield us from something that we worry about and therefore feeds our minds full of crazy information that ultimately decides whether we will do something or not. The imposter creates fearful thoughts, and then our brains will look for evidence to prove them to be true to us.

Some people like to analyse this further and talk about connections to our childhood experiences and analyse those experiences to then justify the reasons for our beliefs, and this is OK to understand why we think the way we do in some cases, but I'm not a person who wants to look backwards rather than thinking forwards. I want to change those limiting beliefs into the ones I want today instead of analysing the past. Events happen in the past, but don't let events dictate your future. *You* dictate it.

What I find fascinating is that these are all around your own beliefs, and this, in turn, comes from your own thoughts, which is fabulous news, as guess what? We can all change our thoughts! I hope you're nodding, as that means you really did read the early chapters!

You may find yourself asking questions or saying statements such as "I don't belong here," "I must get things perfect to justifywhat I'm doing," "What if I fail?" or "What if they find out I'm not as good as they think I am?" *What if, what if, what if, what if?* God, it annoys me so much when my mind starts to challenge me.

The problems these questions can create are things like working harder to try and justify and prove yourself or not making decisions to take that promotion and therefore not living the life or having the career that you want. The lack of progress and feelings of frustration feel like a brick wall at times.

This can lead to feelings of unworthiness and failure that in turn lead to anxiety, depression and burnout. So, it is so important to control the imposter, or it will indeed control you.

There are three steps to dealing with the imposter:

1. Recognise that imposter voice when it appears.
2. Write down what you are thinking and feeling.
3. Question yourself as to whether what you are thinking and feeling is true.

4. If it is not true, then screw up those words into a small package and kick the imposter's ass out into space!
5. Then say in your mind (or out loud if you prefer, depending on who's around), "No thanks, I don't need you today!"

Depending on your answers, you can challenge those beliefs and change them to more empowering beliefs that drive you towards doing what it really is you want to do.

It's very important here to also recognise that some of your thoughts and beliefs may not be your own.

They may be the beliefs of work colleagues that could be challenging your gender, race or old societal expectations, so make sure you really dig deep to understand those imposter thoughts. It could be friends and family thinking they are protecting you. For example, "You don't want that promotion, you'll be too busy and get stressed" or "Women should be at home taking care of the family" or "If you work extra hard and long hours, you'll get paid well" or "Only men really get to the boardroom". The list can go on, so just make sure that the beliefs and values you have are the ones you actually want.

I've heard comments such as, "We don't normally see a woman at these meetings". or "Are you here with your husband?", or "What do you know about an engine?" Whilst I can handle myself and respond to all of those things, when someone makes these kinds of statements, it does make me question myself, and that's when the imposter voice creeps in. Hear something enough times, and you might just start believing it!

Watch out for those negative thoughts that pop into your head.

I usually answer my imposter back by saying, "Thanks for the warning, but now shut up and go away. I've got this!" All right, maybe I swear at it on occasion—OK, I admit it, I swear at it all the time when it shows up. Sometimes it just doesn't listen, so you have to be firm! Thus,

"F**k off out of here, I don't need you!" I'm serious though—give that voice in your head a name so you can say to it, "Thank you for the warning, but I'm OK with this, so shut up", or "I don't believe that anymore. Here's my new thought on this." Then repeat what you really want. It's amazing how you can quiet the doubting mind and that imposter voice so quickly. Give it a go. It may sound daft, but I promise you, it's a really quick way to get that nervous voice out of your head, and you feel much more confident after.

I mentioned Byron Katie earlier, whose best-selling book, *Loving What Is,* has four questions that can change your life and is my go-to guide when I'm challenging beliefs that are holding me back. Use these four key questions to really make sure that your beliefs about what you are thinking are true.

1. Is it true?
2. Are you absolutely sure it's true?
3. How do you react? How do you feel when you believe that thought?
4. Who would you be and how would you feel without that thought?

For example:

"I'm useless at this job." **Is it true?** *Yes,* you answer.

Are you absolutely sure it's true? *Well, I did get the promotion before, and I have launched that new project, but what if I can't do it again and I fail?*

How do you feel when you think that thought? *Worried, scared, anxious.*

Who would you be and feel without that thought? *Creative, organised and with a sense of direction to achieve the new project.*

How does this make you feel? *Confident and empowered.*

Wow, how amazing it is to turn things around in less than a minute! Practise, practise, practise.

When you ask yourself these four questions, it really does challenge you to think deeper, and you have to justify your own answers to yourself! It is critical though that you agree to open up your mind and explore those answers and not be stubborn and say, "Yes, it is true." What if it isn't? What if you are holding yourself back and stopping yourself from having the career, the relationships, and the life you want? Oh my god, how angry and frustrated will you be if you don't realise that you can change this approach?

You will be amazed and fascinated with the conversations you will now uncover with yourself, and this is incredibly powerful. As you challenge yourself, you'll notice that 80% of the time, you find those old beliefs to be untrue.

Do not hold yourself back. You came into this world to live a purposeful, fabulous life, and you can have it. You just need to stop, think and know that there is always a way to achieve anything you want if you learn these tools to help you communicate with yourself and with others.

Stops, pause and think. There is always a way!

Top Tips to Remember

1. Always work out what you want.
2. Focus on what you want and not on what you don't want.
3. Remember your successful moments and focus on the detail of how you felt.
4. Question the doubting mind; are those thoughts true?
5. Ask yourself, does this match your outcome and goals? If not, why not?
6. Turn it around.
7. There is always a way.
8. Never give up.
9. Keep working on your strengths.

Time to Reflect

Write down any of the imposter thoughts you have had or are having. What do they mean? Are they true? Are they *really* true? How do you feel about those thoughts? Who would you be without those thoughts?

_____

_____

_____

_____

_____

_____

_____

_____

_____

_____

_____

_____

_____

CONCLUSION

There's Always a Way—3 Steps to Better Communication

Communication is a learned skill. It takes practice, it takes understanding, and it takes a willingness to rethink how we have been communicating with ourselves and with others. It also takes courage within us to change some things we do that, in the past, we hadn't realised we were doing wrong. This may now explain why you may have felt frustrated in the past that you felt unheard and un-listened-to. Hopefully, this will now change.

Some of the best steps are to create a routine for yourself for when you're faced with moments of challenge.

1. Decide and know what you want.
2. Challenge those beliefs that are getting in the way.
3. Trust and believe that there is always a way.

Ask questions. Seek and you shall find!

In those moments of challenge, whether in a meeting, at the canteen or at home with your children or with your partner, get their feedback and ask questions.

1. Pause, stop talking, zip it and get your emotions in check and decide how you want to react next. Take a deep breath and slow down your

heart rate in case you feel agitated. Remind yourself what it is you want and how you can say it differently or what your next question is to get a better answer or reaction.

2. Smile because you are in control. It can be an internal smile if you don't want to give the wrong impression, but smile on the inside, knowing you are in control of the next step. You are in control of your reactions and your emotions.

3. "There's always a way." Remember this saying, as, in those split seconds, it will jolt your mind into finding the solutions and the right words to say.

4. It's all up to you. Practise, practise, practise. Again, there's always a way!

Once you start to use these steps to help in your communication frustrations, you'll start to see a massive change in your environment. You'll feel less stress, feel more in control and gain fulfilment and enjoyment at work. It is also fascinating how small changes in our behaviour can make such a big difference. Sometimes we have to reflect inward to be able to express outward. You may even find yourself using these tips in your relationships with family and friends, too. Practise, practise, practise and never give up.

It goes without saying, but I'll say it anyway: there are far too many situations in the workplace to cover them all in one book, never mind a short, quick read. I have interviewed many people about this subject and have chosen the most common problems that have come up, and I hope this helps you.

However, there are many more problems that you may need help with but might prefer not to discuss with anyone at work. If this is the case, we can offer you support and find a mentor or a coach to help you. It's worth its weight in gold to have that support and encouragement.

As women, we need to help each other along the way and support each other so that we can improve our lives in our careers, our work environment and our own wellbeing. However, I must now touch on another subject: working with other women!

I have worked mostly in male environments, and when I've discussed this subject with other women who work in male environments, we have all said, "It's far easier to get along with men than it is with women. Why is it that men can have an argument and debate at work and then carry on as normal? If that was two women arguing at work, they wouldn't speak for two weeks!" Why is it that men don't seem to be bitchy or hold grudges, and instead, celebrate each other's successes? Women, on the other hand, are less encouraging. I've also read this in other self-help books, but they don't provide further insight or answers. If you do work it out, drop me a line, would you? This still intrigues me.

What I do know is that if we pull together as women in one direction, we are extremely powerful and strong when supporting and encouraging each other on our journeys. Women do talk more than men, so why don't we use our power and do more of it to create better outcomes for us all, both for the present moment and for our future and future generations to come?

We are all different, we want different career paths and some don't even want a career. So, whatever it is that you want, let's be there for each other and do the best we can. That's the far better, happier and healthier approach.

Theres Always a Way

One thing my father taught me that guides me, drives me and supports me, not only in work but in every area of life: there is always a way!

There are many obstacles in work and in life, and men face them too; we all just need to find a way to deal with them better. My motto in life is that there is "always a way" to do things, solve things and make things right, no matter what the problem is.

As we've discussed, the communication we have with ourselves is indeed more important than that which we have with others; when I tell myself "There's always a way," I know I can find it.

My parents taught me this while I was growing up, and I attribute everything—and I mean everything—in my life to it. The growth of my career, my divorce and the painful loss of my daughter were the three most difficult times in my life, but it was also through those times that I learnt how to "always find a way" to get through any situation, and I've become far stronger, more patient and more appreciative of how our communication is so important in dealing with any situation that we may face, with ourselves and with each other.

I am very passionate about the fact that we should always be learning and growing because if we don't, well, what's the opposite? Learning about how our own minds operate and the very fact that we are indeed in control of our own thoughts is truly incredible when you think about how our own thoughts direct our lives. I lost my daughter and got divorced and I got to choose how to be. I chose control instead of anxiety; I chose to focus on moving forward instead of focusing on panic attacks and depression over things that had happened. I chose my own health instead of medication. I chose exercise instead of the sofa and the TV—but do not get me wrong; now and again, I love a lazy Sunday afternoon watching Netflix with a cup of tea, ginger chocolate cookies and popcorn!

It's your job, your career, your life, your choices and you are responsible for it all, and so it is up to all of us to "find a way." We will always face difficult circumstances, gender inequality, racism and just downright awkward and, in some cases, difficult, horrible people, but there is always a way that we can react, behave and support each other.

We all have a responsibility as women and men to support each other in these circumstances. Cultural change cannot happen in a day, in a week, in a month or, for some of us, in a lifetime, but it all starts with one person. That person is you.

Put on your best coat, smile, say please and thank you. Being polite even in the most difficult moments can be a challenge, but always step up, count to ten and, again, smile.

Seek out a mentor to help you, and don't forget to seek out a *male* mentor. I get tremendous insight from talking to men who also reflect their thoughts on female behaviour. That, quite frankly, is what has helped me to write this book. I have a number of different mentors in my life. Self-reflecting and constant learning are truly the only ways forward, and having a support network around you helps you get there faster.

There's always a way!

So, no matter what, always, always remember—there is always a way!

Everything can be worked out one way or another, so please, if you feel stuck, hopefully, this book helps, and if you need to chat, brainstorm or release the pressure then please do get in touch, no matter what, either with someone you know or with us via our website and social media. www.timefordirecttalk.com #timefordirecttalk.

ONE FINAL NOTE . . .

Like me, you may make mistakes. Learn from them, but *never, ever* let them stop you from having what you want, the job you love and a career to be proud of.

Our lives thrive on how we communicate and interact with each other. It can be just as hard to communicate with other women, our children, our families and our friends as it is to communicate with colleagues, but never give up trying.

When you do use all these tips and that once-difficult conversation is now easy, the feeling is incredible. Doors start to open, stress is less and life feels fabulous.

Let's be amazing together and communicate better.

Time for Direct Talk: it's the conversations we need to have with others, but, more importantly, with ourselves.

Acknowledgements

Thank you to Rob, my partner, who had the patience of a saint whilst I wrote this book. To Phoebe and Hannah, who have given me different perspectives and challenged my own views at times, that allowed me to reflect and think differently and especially to Phoebe, who gave incredible insights from a fourteen-year-old point of view (I think she's going on 40, never mind 14!) which was truly priceless. Thank you, Phoebelicious!

Thank you to all those people, both men and women, who allowed me to interview them for their experiences, their insights and their feedback, which helped the research into this book. Thank you to those who read my book and gave me great feedback, I really appreciate your time.

Thank you to all those who I have worked with, those who really supported me and gave me opportunities. Thank you to those who challenged me and who were downright rude and ignorant to me, as by gosh, it meant I could practise my learnings on you—and it worked!

Thank you to my dad for all that you have taught me and to my sister Sharan for reading this time and time again—you know, one more time just to make sure!

Thank you to Max and Jackson, our two dogs for your cuddles, licks and kisses when I needed them; I'm sorry I was so intense with them!!

About the Author

Sara has spent most of her career in executive management within the food and manufacturing industry. She has worked from Sales Representative to Managing Director, Chairman to Consultant. Sara was awarded a Nuffield Scholarship to research changes in globalisation for the food industry and was the Royal Warrant holder for services to HM the Queen. She has also studied to be a personal and business coach specialising in areas of communication, stress and strategic management. Sara is also a non-executive director.

Sara's passion now is to teach, coach and inspire every single woman to realise that they have everything they need inside of them to live the lives that they want, have the career they desire and learn how to stand up, speak up and be heard.

Sara lives with Rob in Northamptonshire with their two handsome Rotties, Max and Jackson.

Next Steps:

We would love to hear from you about your experiences. Please connect with us via our social media platforms.

Website   www.timefordirecttalk.com

 @timefordirecttalk

 @timefordirecttalk

 @time4directtalk

References

Introduction

Women in Work Index 2021 - PwC UK
Global Gender Gap Report 2021 | World Economic Forum
(weforum.org)

Chapter 1

Albert Mehrabian: nonverbal communication thinker - The British
Library (bl.uk)
www.vark-learn.com
*Mastering Communication at Work: How to Lead, Manage, and
Influence* by Ethan F Becker and Jon Wortmann
Men Are from Mars, Women Are from Venus by John Gray
The 7 Habits of Highly Effective People – Stephen R Covey

Chapter 2

Sex-Dependent Dissociation between Emotional Appraisal and Memory:
A Large-Scale Behavioral and fMRI Study | Journal of Neuroscience
(jneurosci.org)

Chapter 4

NCHS Data Brief, Number 76, October 2011 (cdc.gov)
Why more men than women die by suicide - BBC Future
Mixed feelings: how to deal with emotions at work | Totaljobs

Chapter 5

Women Conductors – Royal Philharmonic Society

Citi becomes first big Wall Street bank to be run by female CEO | Financial Times (ft.com)

Alison Rose to become first female RBS chief executive | Royal Bank of Scotland | The Guardian

Corporate responsibility | Bank of England

Alpha Assertiveness Guide for Men and Women: The Workbook for Training Assertive Behaviour and Communication Skills to Live Bold, Command Respect and Gain Confidence at Work and in Relationships by Gerard Shaw

Chapter 6

Loving What Is by Byron Katie

The 7 Habits of Highly Effective People – Stephen R Covey

Ted Talk – Amy Cuddy 'Power Pose'.

Chapter 7

Equality Act 2010 (legislation.gov.uk)

Recommendation on Preventing and Combating Sexism (coe.int)

Bibliography

Books

- *Alpha Assertiveness Guide for Men and Women: The Workbook for Training Assertive Behaviour and Communication Skills to Live Bold, Command Respect and Gain Confidence at Work and in Relationships* by Gerard Shaw
- *Men Are from Mars, Women Are from Venus* by John Gray
- *The Communication Habit: Strategies That Set You Apart and Leave a Lasting Impression* by Laura Joan Katen
- *Loving What Is* by Byron Katie
- *Mastering Communication at Work: How to Lead, Manage, and Influence* by Ethan F Becker and Jon Wortmann
- *Unlimited Power* by Anthony Robbins
- *Awaken the Giant Within* by Anthony Robbins
- *The High Five Habit* – Mel Robbins
- *The 7 Habits of Highly Effective People* – Stephen R Covey
- *Lean In* – Sheryl Sandberg

YOUR NOTES

Live your life, your way!

YOUR NOTES

You know you can do this; just believe!

YOUR NOTES

I believe in you!

YOUR NOTES

There's always a way – you just have to go and find it. Seek and you shall find.

YOUR NOTES

You are amazing; believe in yourself.

Printed in Great Britain
by Amazon

79542428R00089